Further Praise for *The SELF-Factor:*

"You could change your life with the help of this book! The author has distilled the wisdom of almost 30 years of working with people into a practical, easy to read and well-structured guide to coaching the self. It encourages the reader match the author's approach by being positive and flexible. Charles Handy has recently stressed the importance of 'proper selfishness' not just for individuals but also for organisations and society. Here is a book that shows us how to attain it.

The author demonstrates how we can develop ourselves as a basis for relating better to others and achieving personal meaning in life – and his methods work! I would rate this book alongside Stephen Covey's *7 Habits of Highly Effective People* as one of the best reads for those who are serious about living full, effective and enjoyable lives."

John Wattis, FRC Psych, Professor of Psychiatry of Old Age at the University of Huddersfield, Author of *Practical Psychiatry of Old Age,* coach, mentor and trainer in the NHS.

"This fine book on self-development is the culmination of the author's substantial personal and professional journey. He has done a great job of pulling together a real treasure trove of activities for raising personal awareness. For the person new to this way of being it is a great opportunity to undertake a self-audit with guidance about how to follow through with actions that, in my experience, would definitely produce results. For those – like me, who have experience in this area it is a great reminder of self development activities that we have let slip and maybe become complacent about. 'Self-centred' in the most positive sense."

John Leary Joyce, Founder and CEO of The Academy of Executive Coaching, Director of the Gestalt Centre.

"Duncan is an incredibly powerful and experienced coach. He is also a genuine role model for making the most of potential in a way that is meaningful and aligned with his personal values. Not only could his book change you life and your relationship with yourself, but it is also a great resource for coaches. It can make a dramatic difference to your coaching skills, your impact and the results for your clients."

Carole Gaskell, International Coach, Author of *Transform Your Life* and Founder of the Full Potential Group.

"The SELF-Factor is THE book to help you experience more success and fulfillment – NOW! Written in a way that is easy to understand and fun to implement, it is a comprehensive guide to supporting and coaching yourself to a better life. Duncan's style is very human and motivational and the book makes me excited and enthusiastic to do the self-work to improve my life and my business. The essence of Duncan comes out in his book – honesty, caring, humour, intelligence, authenticity, creativity, understanding, and a deep commitment to supporting people on their life's journey. I wholly recommend his book to everyone who wants to connect with them self and enjoy more success and meaning in their life and work."

Celia Hawe, Yoga Teacher, Life Coach and Author of *Yoga for Slimmers*

"This book has art and heart in abundance. Being so powerfully accompanied by the author makes it a genuinely transformational read. Spiritual intelligence and clear thinking combine to light up the text and distinguish this book from a host of others. Read it!"

Edna Murdoch, Founder of the Coaching Supervision Academy

The SELF-Factor:

The Power of Being You

A Coaching Approach

by

Duncan Coppock

FINDHORN
Press

First published by Findhorn Press 2005

ISBN 1-84409-065-5

British Library Cataloguing-in-Publication Data.
A catalogue record for this book is available from the British Library.

Edited by Kate Keogan
Cover design by Damian Keenan
Printed and bound by WS Bookwell, Finland

Published by

Findhorn Press
305A The Park,
Findhorn, Forres
Scotland IV36 3TE

Tel 01309 690582
Fax 01309 690036
email: info@findhornpress.com

findhornpress.com

Contents

Dedication

This book is dedicated to all those who are ready to be truly themselves and to bring their unique contribution to the world, which needs each and every one of us to play our part.

Acknowledgements

A big thank you to:

All the many teachers, colleagues, practices and organizations that have supported and influenced me over the last thirty years or so.

My family who, in their different ways, have all contributed to who I have become and what I have to say here.

My clients for their willingness to share themselves so openly and their courage to grow. You all teach me so much.

My friends who support me with love, caring, food and laughter – especially when I get too serious.

All at Findhorn Press for believing in this project and supporting me throughout.

John Whitmore for making the time, in his packed schedule, to support me and to write the foreword – a great role model for the coaching community.

And to all those that I have not and may not meet who have and continue to influence me through our shared world. May we all learn to enjoy it and to co-operate together.

Foreword

by John Whitmore

This book fills an important gap in the coaching literature. Many of us have advocated self-coaching, a practice that some coaches often adopt naturally. I go into self-coaching mode every time I put on my skis; awareness, or experiencing the now as it happens, is infinitely more rewarding than the self-instruction and self-criticism with which perfectionists beat themselves up. Few coaches have examined the process of self-coaching fully and none as comprehensively as Duncan has in The SELF-Factor.

However the book goes further than that. There are many instant self-esteem cookbooks on travel bookshop shelves but even the word self-esteem does not imply the value of what I call self-belief, which is what Duncan is referring to. He sets this scene in chapter one so the reader is left with no doubt about the purpose and value of the SELF-Factor.

Self-belief is the life-blood of a good life and the foundation stone on which personal effectiveness stands. It is indispensable for sports performers if they are to get to the top. In 1966 I retired from having been a successful professional racing driver, and paid little attention to the sport thereafter. However in 1990, I was unexpectedly asked to race again and as the big race of the year loomed a couple of hours ahead I felt extremely nervous. It seemed that the value of my whole previous reputation was now to be put to the test. My five year-old son, Jason, scribbled on the hotel notepad a message for me. This is it.

This was before school had had the chance to get at his natural wisdom. For him, I would do anything, so I did what he ordered, confidence filled my being, and I won the race with calm and ease. It was that experience that convinced me just how important the SELF-Factor is and how, when we attend to it, we can become invincible – and I speak less of beating others, than of beating those internal gremlins that so often sabotage us and hold us back from being who we really are, and doing what we really can do.

The SELF-Factor lays out logically and very comprehensively numerous strategies, coaching questions, exercises and anecdotal examples to be used for self-coaching. It includes sections on psychological and physical health, on relationships, on identifying and meeting our own needs, on meaning, purpose and spirituality and on vision and goals. While this is, in the main and importantly so, a book for life and the SELF, at the end it also touches upon the workplace applications of coaching on the SELF-principles.

I have been asked a few times to write about the books of other authors on the subject for which I am best known. I usually find in their pages a number of things with which I disagree, at least in the emphasis or lack of it placed upon certain elements. I have rarely come across any book with which I can so wholeheartedly agree. Only its style differs somewhat from mine. Duncan is more organised and thorough than I am. I am sure that this book will help you on your journey to your SELF.

John Whitmore

John is author of Coaching for Performance *and several other books on learning, development and social change.*

Introduction

I am inviting you now to enrol in an amazing workshop, the ultimate workshop. It's called 'Life'.

One of the amazing things about 'the workshop of life' is that you get to choose at any time, or for any period, what the purpose of the workshop will be. You also get to choose which of the contents you are going to focus on and how much value you will get out of it.

What would you like to take a course in? Material success, having an intimate relationship, leadership, bringing up a family, growing a business, expressing your creativity, excelling in your career? Or perhaps one of the many other subjects available.

And whatever you choose to do, who will you be and how will you be as you do it?

What I am offering here is a foundation course. It allows you, and the people you interact with, to take all the other courses more easily, more happily and more successfully. It also helps you choose future courses that will be more fulfilling and life-affirming, rather than being enrolled in whatever comes along by default.

Together we are going to explore a course in fully appreciating your greatest asset, yourself. My experience, of working with people for almost thirty years, is that at the core of us all there is a common source of wisdom, strength and joy coupled with a desire to live a meaningful life and to contribute to our world. In this respect we are all the same. Alongside that, we each have our own unique combination of values, talents, style and quirks, all of which contribute to the rich tapestry of our lives together. The more that you can tap into your inner strength AND embrace your own and others' humanness, the more you will have the power to create a meaningful and happy life. This is the power that comes from being you.

The extent to which you can tap into this power depends upon your relationship with yourself. The way that you see, behave towards and express yourself is the biggest single factor in determining who you will allow yourself to be, what you will allow yourself to do and to have, and how you will perceive and experience life. Your relationship with yourself is also the basis for good relationships with others.

Wherever you are, whatever you do and whatever you say, your effectiveness will always depend on the you who is there, doing and saying. This is what I call the self-factor. For both individuals and organizations, the self-factor is the foundation on which all success is built. Even more importantly, developing a strong relationship with and sense of self is crucial to your feeling fulfilled in your life and work.

You are not omnipotent and the best sense of self in the world does not guarantee that there will be no disasters or disappointments or that you will accomplish everything that you want to. It will, however, enable you to make the most of your time, talents and opportunities. Considering that most of us use only a fraction of our potential, this is a huge shift.

A few years ago, I was involved in a series of trainings for Australian Telecom, which involved everyone from top management to call operators. On every level, the thing that people most reported wanting more of was appreciation. There have been numerous studies that have confirmed this and shown that when people are appreciated they are more committed, resourceful and effective.

From my dictionary, the three main definitions of 'to appreciate' are:

- To value highly and be grateful for
- To be aware of and understand
- To develop in value

Don't you want more of this in your work and relationships? And if you want it from others, who are around you for just a part of the time, then realize how much more important it is that you give it to yourself — because you are there with you all of the time.

If you are a coach or other professional using coaching

In the book, you will find an abundance of ideas, models and tools that have been used very successfully by myself and by coaches that I have trained and mentored. When I introduce new ideas to coaches, I always start by having the coaches apply them to themselves so that they integrate them into their own lives before using them with clients. Then their coaching conversations have authenticity and clients are far more likely to open up and to trust them.

If you are a leader or manager

It is becoming more common now to speak of people as being your greatest asset. Apart from the ethical aspects involved, the financial and other costs of burn out, low morale and high staff turnover are escalating. You can use the ideas in this book in two ways. Firstly, to take care of and empower yourself, so that you are in a more resourceful state and can model the way. Secondly, as a guide on how to appreciate and support your teams and employees. If, however, you try to do the second without the first then you are likely to have little impact.

If you are a teacher or parent

The same is true when dealing with children. If you want them to develop high self-esteem and self-care, then remember that they learn most by imitation.

For these reasons, whatever your role, this book is mostly written from the standpoint of applying the principles to yourself. From your own experience of walking your talk you can then support others.

There can be a great reluctance to appreciate and take care of yourself, as if this were somehow selfish or taking away from others. In practice it is the basis for healthy synergistic relationships. It is like the safety message on an aircraft where you are told to fit your own oxygen mask before attempting to help anyone else. When you are taken care of then you can be of real benefit to others.

Our inner and outer worlds reflect each other. At the deepest level, learning to appreciate yourself is about developing a rich, ongoing relationship with life. It is a journey of discovery and no one can travel the road for you. My intention is to make your journey a little lighter, by discarding some unnecessary baggage, and to make your route more direct by providing some outline maps of the territory. The examples I give are simple enough for you to use immediately and flexible enough for you to make them your own. As your understanding and experience of the process grows, I encourage you to periodically re-draw the maps to fit your unique perspective and requirements.

My style of coaching, whether personal or business, is about making the most of potential and opportunities in ways that are meaningful and aligned with your values. The best coaches are masters at supporting their clients in learning to appreciate themselves more. Where coaching differs from some other approaches is that it occurs in the context of fully owning, engaging in, and taking action in your life.

It's in this context that I invite you to appreciate and strengthen your relationship with yourself. You can try out new behaviours, take care of your needs, develop a more positive attitude and learn to support yourself unconditionally. You can engage in a dance of learning through interaction and reflection.

A game worth playing

One deeply held myth in our current society is that of the perfectly happy, healthy and successful person. It is an expectation that in our life, career and relationships we can, and indeed should, have it all, all of the time. If we don't manage to achieve this then we feel that something has gone drastically wrong and that we have failed. In extreme contrast to the perfect-life myth is a belief that we are helpless victims of upbringing, society and circumstance, condemned to endure whatever life has given us.

The reality is that most of us do grossly under-use our ability to make choices and improve our experience AND that sometimes life is messy and difficult and doesn't fit the storybooks AND that we always have a choice in how we respond to it.

This or any other book cannot make you okay, for the simple reason that you already are okay. In fact you are more than okay, you are unique. From that perspective you can afford to experiment, express yourself and make the best of what is possible. Then you get to play an entirely different game with the odds stacked in your favour.

And that is the game in which I invite you to join me. It is a game where you can be real and human and can afford to take risks because whether things work out or not, you are still okay. I invite you to have a relationship, a lifelong love affair, with yourself.

I am playing the game myself and, yes, sometimes I still have 'bad me' days. That is how real relationships are; they involve challenges as well as joy, require commitment and working on, and they deepen over time. The difference with this relationship is that, like it or not, it is 24/7 and here for life. Divorce is not an option!

Make it your game and adjust the rules to work for you. If you're ready to join the workshop, then it's time to begin ...

I ~ Setting the Scene

My overall purpose is to support you in:

- Feeling good in, and about, yourself
- Being authentic and expressing yourself fully
- Making the most of your life, work and opportunities
- Making a positive contribution to the people and world around you

You can use these points as criteria for how you understand or use the different models introduced in the book. If an idea doesn't support you in these areas then adapt it or dump it. Please don't use it to undermine yourself or your life.

As a coach, I work with a wide variety of clients. I will support you whether you want to be the best beach-bum in the world, lead your organization to the next level, do a satisfying day's work for reasonable pay, advance your career, compose music, be a better parent, or whatever. My concern is that, whatever you are involved in, it is meaningful and important to you, allows you to be authentic and supports you in feeling good in, and about, yourself.

Whoever you are, and whatever you do, the relationship with yourself will be the biggest single factor in determining how happy and effective you will be.

Fulfilment beyond success

Coaches have traditionally supported clients in being more effective and achieving their goals. In recent years, more and more clients are additionally talking about wanting to live fuller lives and to find more meaning in what they do. They are finding that conventional success is not always deeply satisfying or worth the cost to their lives as a whole.

Being fulfilled is about much more than achieving a set of goals or getting gold stars from people around you. It is about how you do things as well as what you do. It is about being yourself and choosing aims and methods that matter to you. It is about being with integrity so that who you are aligns with what you say and what you do.

All of this depends on having a strong relationship with yourself — one which enables you to connect with and express the power within you and, at the same time, allows you to embrace your everyday humanness.

The SELF model

The SELF model is a set of ideas and tools for connecting with, supporting and expressing yourself fully. It is for people, like you, who want to get more out of life than simply getting by. Many people admit that they can be their own worst enemy. The approaches contained in the SELF model will help you to become your own best friend.

Individuals coming to coaching want to feel better about themselves and to get more out of their lives and work. Organizations using coaching want to motivate and inspire their managers and executives to produce better results and to build better teams. In all coaching lasting success requires that you appreciate and support yourself more fully as a person rather than just as a commodity. It requires that you connect with, and take care of, yourself, and that you achieve your aims from a place of greater resourcefulness and satisfaction.

Only a limited number of people get to work with a coach and not all coaches are skilled in this deeper and necessary adjunct to working with particular goals and projects. Having worked with and trained hundreds of coaches and clients, I continually hear how good it feels to be fully accepted, given permission to tell the truth of how things are, warts and all, AND to be encouraged and supported in recognising your potential and in aiming for more. That is how we will work together in this book.

Just as the different plants and trees in a garden have their special foliage, scents and fruits, so you have your own individual character, essence, and contribution for the world. Plants and trees thrive when looked after and nourished. In the same way, you need the right conditions for you to flourish. The SELF model is a guide to providing the conditions under which you can grow and be your best. It is an outline for what a self needs to be healthy, happy, effective and fulfilled.

The four aspects of the SELF model

S ustaining
E mpowering
L istening
F riendship

Sustaining is about providing yourself with a nourishing and safe environment and doing what it takes for your various needs to be taken care of. Unmet needs tend to drive you, make you cranky and drain your energy. Meeting your needs in a healthy way gives you energy and a foundation for relating well with others.

Empowering is about believing in, encouraging and supporting yourself so that you have the best chance of achieving the things that really matter to you. It involves taking responsibility for your self and your life as well as creating a positive mental and emotional climate in which you can grow and move forward. It also means providing yourself with the necessary time, and other resources, for whatever you undertake.

Listening is about taking the time to acknowledge what is true for you on different levels. It is about finding out what your values are and what you really care about and want. Many of us lead such busy lives that we are out of touch with ourselves and cannot see the wood for the trees. When you slow down and connect with yourself, then you have access to much greater wisdom and perspective.

Friendship is about giving yourself the gift of unconditional, positive regard so that whatever is going on in your life, and however you are doing, you are always there for you and ready to support yourself. Friendship is the overview that both informs the other elements and is developed by them. If you are to take only one thing from this book, then make it the intention to be a really good friend to yourself.

There is an enormous power that comes from fully being you. The four parts of the SELF model help you to access and express that power, in different ways.

Each of the four aspects will be explored in greater depth in its own chapter. Once you are familiar with them, they can be used together because they interlink and mutually support each other. As you take care of your needs and sustain yourself more this will empower you and create more space in which to listen to your self. As you listen with friendship rather than judgement, you create a safer space in which to acknowledge your needs and to take the necessary steps towards meeting them. You also make it safer to take risks, to extend your comfort zone and to make more of your opportunities, – all of which is highly empowering. As you feel more empowered, you learn to take responsibility for your experiences and are much more able to make supportive changes.

So, shifts in any one aspect will bring about shifts in the others and your journey towards fully appreciating and expressing yourself will be unique to you. You can also apply the ideas as you support and respect others, whether they are clients, friends, family, or people that you influence as part of your job.

Being your own coach

This book is written from a coaching perspective. Coaching, as I view it, is not prescriptive. The coach acts as a catalyst and the power comes from engaging together in a deep exploration of your particular situation. You remain the authority on what is right for you. As a coach, my job is not to tell you or anybody else how to think or how to live. My purpose is to support you in raising your awareness and in taking responsibility so that you are better equipped to choose for yourself.

In that light, as you read this book, I encourage you to be your own coach. Use the different suggestions to get you thinking and to shine the spotlight of awareness on your own life and work. Explore the various ideas and then decide what does and does not work for you. There will be a difference in how much you get out of the book, depending on whether you scan through it quickly or whether you really take the time to reflect and think for yourself. Roughly speaking, your response to the different ideas will fall into one of three categories:

- You will know intuitively that something is right for you – so apply it
- You will know intuitively that something is not right for you – so ignore it
- You will need to try something out before knowing – so experiment with it

The last category will be the largest. Give yourself the chance to try things out, to see what works and to adjust ideas to suit you.

Reflection points

To help you think and choose for yourself, you will find 'reflection points' throughout the book. These provide an opportunity for you to pause and to reflect on what happens and what is possible for you. You may also like to write about an idea or discuss it with a friend.

Reflection point **Your relationship with yourself**

In what ways do you have a good relationship with yourself now and in what ways could you improve on it?

If your style and preference is to scan the chapters quickly and to try out some tools then that is also valid and possible. At the end of most of the chapters you will find key points, intentions to hold and possible actions steps. These are a starting point from which you can create your own intentions and actions that more fully reflect your unique perspective and needs.

The discussion and reflections points are designed to raise your awareness of current reality as well as how else you might want things to be. Change is then fuelled with intention and developed through action. Action brings feedback from which you can learn, gain more awareness, re-direct your intention and take further action. This process continues until you achieve your desired outcomes or else choose something else.

Holding an intention

As it is used in the chapter summaries, holding an intention means having a focus and a vision of how you want things to be. For instance, you may hold the intention to live more healthily. This in itself can be powerful if it is consistently kept in your awareness. One way of keeping your intention alive is, twice per day, to subjectively score yourself out of ten for how much the intention was maintained, and to notice what did and did not help. Don't judge yourself as you do this. Developing an increased awareness of how things are going, and what is involved, will already be a catalyst for change. If you are visually-oriented, then you may want to make a chart and to stick it up where you will see it frequently. Writing about your experience or sharing it with others, for support, can also be very helpful.

Taking action

Alongside holding the intention, you can choose to commit to specific goals and action steps. For instance, joining a weight-loss club or taking regular exercise as part of a sustainable life-style. While different people respond to different degrees of detail, most will benefit from committing to some specific actions. From the suggested intentions and actions at the end of each chapter, choose just two or three of each. Better still, come up with some of your own.

Chapter 7 gives an overview of working with vision, intentions and goals. You may like to glance at that alongside working through the other chapters.

You will also find throughout the book various case studies that illustrate the application of some of the ideas.

As we journey together, I am going to suggest that you change some of the ways in which you relate to yourself and your life – not only in what you do, but in how you think and feel, and how you look at things. The next chapter is a reference chapter which draws a map of the territory, explains what is involved and prepares you for creating or responding to change in general.

2 ~ Changing for a Change

This chapter introduces some recurring themes that we will be dealing with directly or indirectly many times. You can read it through quickly now to get an overview of what is involved and then refer to it, as needed, as you go through the rest of the book.

Want it or not, life is changing dramatically these days. It used to be that people boarded a symbolic train, with career and relationship, and stayed on that train as it travelled down the preset tracks of time. There were upsets and challenges on the way but relatively few decisions to make about the destination or the route. Changes of track were signalled well ahead so that points could be set and any curves smoothed out. Sure there were hard times but they took place in the context of knowing that you belonged with your train and your long-term fellow passengers. Along with that, your parents and school knew what career was best for you, the church provided you with answers about morality and your doctor knew what was best for your health.

Now change is becoming a constant. You no longer have to stay in a difficult relationship or job just because that is what you are supposed to do. The general trend is towards a series of relationships and careers. Even if you are disposed to settling for what you have there is no guarantee that your partner will not leave or that your company won't downsize. People change locations more frequently and the support of an extended family nearby is less common. At the same time our faith in the experts' knowing what is best for us has been irreparably shaken.

While not all of these changes in society may be for the good, the reality is that they have occurred and you have to deal with them. The overall result is that you cannot, as before, rely on others for your sense of identity or for your choices. The downside is that all this change and unpredictably can be stressful and unsettling. The upside is that the same challenges can lead to your becoming more aware and give you new possibilities.

One very important factor in how you initiate or respond to change is the beliefs from which you operate.

The way beliefs work

Your beliefs tell you how things should be; they have an amazingly strong influence upon your life. Beliefs are ideas that have feelings, and a certain way of looking at things, associated with them. Together these form your attitudes to yourself, to life and to whatever outcomes you aspire to.

They tell you who to be, how to communicate and how to act. As a result, you attract and notice particular people and situations and have experiences that fit with your expectations. All of this provides 'evidence' that reinforces the belief and the cycle continues. (See the diagram opposite.) In time a belief is accepted as 'the truth' and, if shared by enough other people, can even be considered 'a fact of life'. Beliefs can be positive and life-affirming or they can be negative and limiting; people who say they can and people who say they can't are generally both right.

Particular techniques for working with limiting beliefs will be explored more fully in chapter 4, as part of empowering yourself. Here we look at how they are maintained and how they are involved in the general process of change.

The reaction cycle

Established beliefs are maintained and operated by unconscious habit. If they are positive and supportive then all is well and there is no need to fix what isn't broken. Frequently, though, we develop belief cycles that are limiting and unsupportive and we become trapped in a cycle of reaction. We react to the 'evidence' of our experience by re-affirming our beliefs about how things are. What we put out in the world is a reaction to these beliefs. The world around us reacts to what we are putting out and gives us more of the same 'evidence'. And so it continues with unconscious reaction, rather than love, making the cycle go round and round.

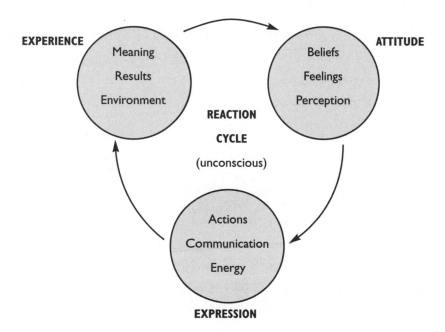

Living in the comfort zone

All of this makes us experts at doing things the way we always do them. Most of the time we operate on automatic and our unconscious mind quietly carries out its programming and perpetuates the known, for good or bad. We stay within our comfort zone. Our 'comfort zone' may actually involve a lot of pain and struggle, but it is familiar and that makes it relatively comfortable and predictable. The unconscious logic goes something like this: 'Look, honey, doing what we've always done at least we're still here; we've survived. If we do something different then God knows what might happen!'

Your old belief/reaction cycles work to maintain the status quo so that if you start to move outside your familiar ways of doing things then you are likely to feel anxiety and doubt. Your unconscious feels you are under threat and will attempt to bring you back to the 'safety' of the established comfort zone as soon as possible.

Reflection point **Stepping outside your comfort zone**

What things would you like to try but don't because it would mean stepping outside your comfort zone?

The force of habit

To get an idea of how strongly your way of doing things is held in place, let's try an experiment. Read through the following instructions and then put the book down and try them out.

First, fold your arms the way you normally do and notice which arm is on top. Are you a lefty or a righty? Then quickly bring your hands down, slap your thighs and fold your arms the opposite way. Check that you really do have the other arm on top and notice how it feels.

How did you get on? Did you find it easy? Did it feel comfortable?

When I do this with groups it is usually around half and half which arm is on top. And it doesn't seem to correlate with whether people are left- or right-handed. It is just a habit. If you found it easy, then congratulations. If you found it tricky, then you are in the majority. For most people, folding their arms the opposite way is challenging and feels unnatural and even 'wrong'. So it is when changing most habits. The first obstacle is the dominance of the established way of doing things. The second obstacle is that the new way initially feels wrong.

Now, if you were to choose to fold your arms consistently this way over the next month, then how do you think it would feel?

It would probably feel fine and become established as a new habit.

And so it is with many habits and belief cycles. If you consciously and consistently practise a new way then it can become established as a positive habit. But first you may need to be willing to experience some short-term discomfort.

PERSONAL CASE STUDY ~ CHANGING A HABIT

I had a strong lisp up to the age of thirty. I had avoided using my voice in my performance work and played it safe by being more movement based. At that point I made the decision to change and started lessons with a speech therapist who showed me how to speak without the lisp. She also encouraged me to go through the short term discomfort until the new tongue positions became established as a positive habit.

Reflection point **Short-term discomfort**

Can you think of a positive habit that you would like to establish?

Are you willing to put up with a little short-term discomfort?

Self-sabotage

If you think of your resistance to change as an inner saboteur or a sign of weakness, then you will be inclined to struggle with, and try to overpower, yourself. This is hard work, especially as struggling with the pattern gives it more energy! If you can appreciate that the underlying intention of your resistance is for your (albeit misperceived) well-being, then change can still be a challenge but you can look for creative ways to get your unconscious mind working more onside with you.

Characters and scripts

Shakespeare said: 'All the world's a stage and all the men and women merely players.'

As noted earlier, change is becoming a constant in life whether we choose it or not. The problem is that much of the time, even though we change relationships, jobs and locations, we still operate from the same old belief/reaction cycles. So we maintain our habitual ways of thinking and doing things. It is as if we are a character in a play who is introduced to new people and situations and reacts to them as he or she normally reacts to people and situations. Bit by bit the old scenes are recreated with different backdrops. Or, to use another metaphor, you may acquire some new wine but then store it in old wineskins.

When you change your self-image and belief patterns it is as if you rewrite your character and way of responding to the world. And then, even with the same people and situations, you can experience and respond to them differently.

PERSONAL CASE STUDY, CONTINUED

Initially after learning to speak without a lisp I was still hesitant and insecure about my voice. I then found a wonderful drama coach who inspired me to think of myself as someone who had a good speaking and singing voice – to be someone with a good voice. Now, years later, my voice is still one of my major strengths which I use in all my phone work and also for guided visualizations with groups.

To a certain extent all roles are illusory and your true identity is closer to that of the author, writing both character and script. Nevertheless, you do take on roles and it makes sense to have them more clearly reflect your essential nature as loving, creative, joyful and sharing.

Reflection point **Role-playing**

What identity or role would you like to try out, maybe just for an evening to start with?

Consciousness and change

Consciousness is the human birthright that allows you to choose from a far greater range of possibilities in life than any other animal can. A baby deer is able to walk within a few hours of birth because how to do so is hard-wired into its nervous system. A baby human has to learn to walk over a year or two and to establish the neuro-connections bit by bit. A rough deal, you might think! But a human can then go on to play a violin, program a computer, play tennis, write a sonnet or do millions of activities that no other animal can aspire to. With choice comes responsibility and you are also free, if you choose, to develop destructive postures and movement and negative attitudes. It's all part of the deal.

The good news is that, at any time, you can consciously choose to re-program yourself.

Aspects of consciousness

- Acceptance
- Awareness
- Intention
- Learning

The bottom line is that if you are not aware of something then you don't have any choice about it. So developing awareness is essential. However, if you don't have a basic attitude of self-acceptance then looking at yourself is going to be a very painful and limited process – lots of 'Oh my God, I'm not really like that. No way. That's the other guy.' It is even harder when the other guy is one of your parents … or your partner!

There is a lovely Buddhist mudra, or hand position, used for meditation. The right hand, representing awareness, is held in the left hand representing compassion. Unless you create a safe and accepting space, people will not willingly share or reveal themselves. The same is true of observing yourself, your thoughts and your behaviour. Without acceptance, awareness will be limited.

Acceptance and awareness bring about understanding. But understanding without action can be the booby prize – 'Hey, I used to have all these negative habits without even knowing about them. Now I know *all* about them … .' On the other hand, action without acceptance is dire. Never mind how much you change, you will never feel satisfied. So positive change involves a healthy balance of acceptance and intention to change, grounded in action.

Intention is how you formulate and energize your choices. There is a strong emphasis in this book on self-acceptance and appreciation. However, out of that acceptance, you will almost certainly want to make more good things happen in your life because you know that you want and deserve them. You will also want to make a meaningful contribution to your world. This requires intention. It can be directed towards a very specific goal using sustained willpower or it can be directed to a more flexible vision using a looser and creative approach. And then again it can be a combination of the two.

Learning is the wonderful ability to grow and develop new skills, qualities and perspectives throughout your life, and to adapt to feedback from anything that you do. I also believe that it keeps you feeling younger and energized. When I got to forty, I started to look for role models of older people who enjoyed life. I noticed that musicians and conductors did pretty well and it struck me that they were always learning, being creative and interacting with people. So I've become a life-long learner. Of course, if you keep forgetting things as much as I do then that is relatively easy! Many books on positive thinking say you shouldn't make that kind of joke against yourself, but I guess I'm a bit of a risk-taker as I get older. I'll be getting a leather bike-suit and a Harley Davidson with a heated seat next ....

Intuition and logic

Many times being conscious is thought of as being rational. Logical thinking is a wonderful resource and yet you have access to far more wisdom and insight than that provided by logic alone. You may think of this as intuition or you may experience it as tuning in, listening to your heart, your higher self or whatever works for you. You may also link it to your notion of God or spirituality.

Whatever words you use, the point is that when you slow down, become conscious and connect inside, then you are able to make better decisions and to draw on another kind of wisdom, strength and intention than you can reach with logical thinking alone. Consciousness draws on both intuition and rational thinking. When they work well then they complement each other.

A unified approach to change

In this book we take a unified approach to change – bringing all aspects of consciousness to bear on the full belief cycle and re-writing character as well as script.

The creation cycle

Write the word 'REACTION' in capital letters on a piece of paper. Now cross out the 'C' in the middle and insert it at the beginning instead. What do you get?

Lo and behold, when you start off with 'C-ing' where you are and where you want to go then you move from REACTION to CREATION. This represents bringing consciousness to the forefront. When you do this, the reaction cycle becomes the creation cycle.

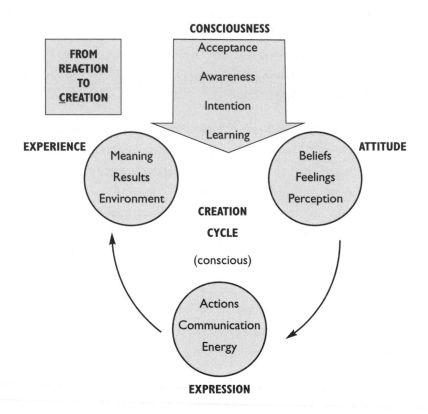

Applying this to change

- You can bring all aspects of consciousness to bear on yourself and your life.

- First of all, approach yourself within an overall atmosphere of self-acceptance and knowing that you are okay.

- Then develop an attitude of appreciative curiosity about yourself and life and shine the spotlight of your awareness on whatever you are involved in.

- Exercise your intention, trying out different strategies and seeing what happens.

- Learn from whatever happens and be willing to adapt and to develop.

Applying this to all parts of the belief cycle

- Life-affirming attitudes can be developed, with positive thoughts supported by feelings of expectation and by seeing the possibilities in life.

- You can 'act as if' and explore different behaviours that align with how you want things to be. You can also experiment with how you communicate and with the general vibe that you put out in the world.

- You can choose to have supportive environments and people around you. Notice and learn from the results you produce and emphasize the evidence for things getting better.

And finally, you can realize that, being human, you will always be in process and learning, which brings us back to the need for acceptance.

This unified approach can be applied to any goal or area of your life; in the coaching process, we weave in different parts of it as they naturally occur. Bit by bit you assimilate the approach as a whole and find yourself more positive, empowered, happy and successful.

In later chapters there will be particular emphasis and practice on working with beliefs, trying out new behaviours, creating a nurturing environment, listening more fully to your own truth and wisdom, and on other aspects touched on in this chapter. This has been a brief overview to see how they all fit together. You may like to return to it from time to time.

3 ~ Sustaining Your Self

Overview

Part of what gives you personal power is embracing your everyday humanness. We are now going to look at what it takes to sustain yourself for the duration of a project and, in the bigger picture, for a long, healthy and happy life.

The vision

I have a vision of you living a vibrant life in which you give freely from a place of health and abundance. For this to happen, you need to value yourself and your contribution sufficiently to take really good care of yourself. It is like preparing for an exciting road journey and making sure that the car is first serviced and in good order.

Sustaining is not just about survival and taking care of yourself is not an end in itself. I don't encourage a 'me, me, me!' culture because I don't think that really makes you happy. We are talking about what it takes for you to live your life to the full, including experiencing the fulfilment that comes from contributing freely and meaningfully to the people and the world around you.

What do we mean by sustaining?

Relevant definitions are:

Sustaining:
- *keeping up the vitality or strength of*
- *providing sustenance or nourishment*

Sustainability: • *using a resource so that the resource is not depleted or permanently damaged*
    • *relating to a lifestyle involving the use of sustainable methods*

You are going to focus on taking care of your natural resources and getting your various needs met so that you are both nourished and effective. You will also look at increasing your sources of positive energy and reducing energy drains. As you do all of this, you will feel better and more satisfied in yourself and can then, in turn, give the world a better you.

Reflection point   **If you carry on living the way you do now**

How sustainable is your present way of living?

If you carry on living as you are now, how do you expect to feel:

- *in 6 months' time?*
- *in 3 years' time?*
- *in 20 years' time?*

Sustainability requires a commitment to self-care, which is not the same as being selfish. Treating yourself well and with respect, creating a nourishing personal environment and choosing, where possible, to be happy and fulfilled results in a more resourceful and energized you. When you are well taken care of, you are more able to healthily support and contribute to others. Then whatever you choose to give is more likely to be given freely and gladly, rather than with a sense of personal sacrifice and resentment.

Or we can turn it round the other way; when you don't feel safe and nourished by your environment, you are more likely to be defensive or aggressive. And if you don't get your needs met then you are far more likely to be awkward and a general pain in the butt! If you find yourself frequently getting cranky with other people then it is a good idea to ask yourself which of your needs are not being met.

Different perspectives on sustainability

We can look at sustainability through the filters of different perspectives that overlap and mutually support each other. These include:

- Personal ecology
- Taking care of your needs
- Energy maintenance

Personal ecology

You as a part of nature

Sustainability, of the environment and our shared natural resources, is thankfully becoming recognized as a mainstream, urgent concern. Individuals, groups and nations are starting to work together to address the critical problems that unconscious short-term living, irresponsible growth and consumerism have created for our planet, nature and ourselves.

You and your body are the nearest point of nature and your own natural resources also need to be respected and well used. You have a personal responsibility to set things up so that you operate from healthy, renewable sources of energy rather than living off adrenalin, which is unsustainable and leads to stress and burn-out. There is only one of you and, in the entire history of humankind, you will never again be repeated. Do you have a reverence for this unique gift of life that you have been given? Or are you putting your head in the sand and turning yourself into an endangered species?!

Getting off the treadmill

You may now be saying your equivalent of 'Ah, but if you only knew my life, then you would know that it is simply not possible to take better care of myself. So many demands at work and at home! If I didn't keep going flat out then it would all go down the drain.'

It seems like you are truly indispensable. Send for the t-shirt, do not pass Go, do not collect £200 and above all do not stop! Yet as a friend of mine said, 'Isn't it strange how many "indispensable" people you can find in the graveyard?' And isn't it even stranger that, when an indispensable person dies, whoever is left behind somehow carries on without them?

Let's be honest and acknowledge that some people do indeed have a tougher life and more non-negotiable variables than other people. I don't want to trivialize the genuine hardships, challenges and demands that can occur in life. Some carers and other people keep going under extreme conditions. Where necessary, you may have to accept and deal with, as cheerfully as possible, some pain and limitation. In that case, acceptance can be the healthiest option – provided that, where possible, you have a strong preference for, and actively choose, abundance and happiness.

For many, if not most, of my clients, their problems have as much (or more) to do with the choices they make as with the external circumstances. As you look at your own life, is it really true that you couldn't take better care of, and be more supportive of yourself, if you made it important enough?

It can be helpful to examine your priorities and to ask yourself what, in your present life, you could let go of in order to give yourself more of what you need to be a more happy, healthy and resourceful you. I often find that people are resistant even to considering letting go of anything and will argue vehemently that there is nothing that could be changed. And yet, when an unforeseen emergency happens, all sorts of things get dropped which had previously been considered non-negotiable 'have to happen' activities.

Illness and other emergencies are often the catalyst for change and it is quite common for survivors of cancer and other life-threatening diseases to speak about the new perspectives and priorities that dealing with their challenge has helped them to develop. How much better would it be to look at and re-organize your priorities without simultaneously having to deal with the fear and stress of going through a life-threatening illness?

Reflection point **What can you let go of?**

Suppose that an illness or other emergency happened and that you had no option but to give up two days per week of your time to deal with it.

What would be the first things, in your present schedule, that you would let go of?

Talking through this imaginary scenario with a friend or a coach can be a powerful way of examining your priorities and starting to organize your life to be more sustainable.

Adrenalin junkies

One of the ways in which we squander our natural energy reserves is through over-reliance on adrenalin. In the short term we often end up driving through projects, shelving our needs and getting by on adrenalin. In exceptional circumstances this may be necessary but if you turn this into a way of living then your health and quality of life are severely affected. Ongoing reliance on adrenalin becomes an addiction and, like other addictions, is not always obvious when you are in the midst of it. It is only when you remove yourself from the situation and the stress that you wonder what you were doing and see the cost; life has been going by while you were too busy to enjoy it.

In the long term you want to develop a more sustainable and happier way of motivating yourself and carrying things out. Start to think of yourself as a complex eco-system interacting with, and part of, other eco-systems.

Reflection point **Becoming more personally eco-friendly**

How sustainable is the way you are living your life?

What needs to change for you to become more personally eco-friendly?

Understanding your needs

We all have different needs which, if not met, undermine our sense of self and the way in which we show up in the world. Sometimes there can be an understandable reluctance to admit to our needs out of the fear of becoming 'needy'. Having needs is not the problem – that's just a part of being human. It is how we think about those needs and how we do, or do not, deal with them that causes problems. Pretending that we don't have needs is a denial of our humanness and leads to our being judgemental of ourselves and of other people. When we embrace all of our humanness – including our talents, values, needs and foibles – we came across as real and authentic and it adds to our personal power.

So what are your needs?

Relevant definitions of 'need' are:

- *a physiological or psychological requirement for the well-being of an organism*
- *a lack of something requisite, desirable, or useful*

Depending on which definition is being emphasized, this leads to different views on, and ways of dealing with, needs in general. The first definition suggests that there are needs that have to be met or else you, as an organism, will necessarily suffer. The second definition suggests the possibility of needs that, while not actual requirements, are nevertheless desirable or useful and make life easier. It is helpful to get clearer on when a particular need is a requirement for you, and when it is something desirable or useful but not immediately essential.

Animals will endure hardship and lack of food, when necessary, but will actively seek the best conditions where possible. You don't find a hungry lion ignoring passing prey and she will choose the warm sunshine over crouching in the gloom – unless of course she gets a better signal on the mobile phone there. In the same way, a healthy individual will accept pain and limitations, when necessary, and yet have a strong preference for ease, happiness and abundance. It is like climbing a mountain with a rucksack full of rocks on your back. It is possible and occasionally, as a training exercise, it might even be character building. But if you want to climb a lot of mountains then it makes sense to get your needs met and dump the rocks!

At the other end of the spectrum, there are examples of individuals who seem to have more than enough on the material level and never progress further. It is as if their thermostat is broken and the drive for more possessions and for recognition from others never gets shut off. If you find yourself driven, with a faulty thermostat, then you may need to look at how much is really enough and whether the original need has become more of a dysfunctional habit.

Most of what we will be talking about here are not life-and-death survival needs; to treat them as such can leave you feeling disempowered and needy. It is, though, very important to realize that you have a variety of different needs that, if not acknowledged and met, tend to drive your behaviour and leave you less happy, resourceful and effective than you could be. Unacknowledged and unmet needs also tend to make you crankier and less fun to be around.

As human beings we have certain needs in common – such as to survive, to belong and to relate. There are also some shared principles – such as honesty, fairness, justice and equality – which seem fundamental to any healthy society. Alongside shared needs and principles, you also have your own particular needs, preferences, style and values. These are part of what makes you uniquely who you are and you will want to take them fully into account where possible. For instance, in a relationship, it may be important for you to be with someone who is fun-loving and outgoing. While this might not be a life-or-death necessity, it makes sense to take your particular needs and values into account when choosing a prospective mate.

Different approaches to needs

Seeing needs as essential

Some personal development approaches emphasize getting your foundation needs met as an essential pre-requisite to further growth. The upside of this approach is that you get to put self-care at the top of your list of priorities, which can help you to become stronger with a more solid foundation. The downside is that you can become overly concerned with needs that are currently not met and then think that you have to meet them all fully (as determined by somebody else's criteria) before you can be happy, productive and generally okay.

Practising self-reliance

At the other end of the personal development spectrum, some practitioners and teachers take a more 'kick arse' approach to developing self-reliance and eliminating neediness. From this point of view, apart from life-and-death survival needs, everything else is a preference. Saying that you 'need' something, rather than that you would like it, is undermining and can make you unnecessarily unhappy, dependent and needy. The upside of this approach is that it can help you become more self-reliant and go-getting. The downside is that you can become physically and emotionally rigid and out of touch with your body and your feelings. It can also lead to your using achievements as compensations for dissatisfaction with other areas of your life.

Needs and the spiritual perspective

There are also different perspectives on spirituality in relation to your humanness and your needs. Some view physical needs and the desire for self-achievement as obstacles to communion with God or enlightenment. Hence they emphasize denial or subjugation of the body and the ego as signs of spiritual advancement.

At the other end of the spiritual spectrum, some New Age teachers promote a kind of 'spirituality of success' philosophy. They imply that the correct mind-set and practices lead automatically to material and interpersonal abundance – with the pernicious reverse implication that if you are struggling or lacking in some area then you cannot be properly spiritual.

Bringing it all together

All of these approaches seem to appeal to, and to help, some people some of the time. So where do you start and how do you choose between them? I am still waiting for the secret 'Duncan Manual' to be found in a cave somewhere that tells me exactly how to operate this complicated person called me. In the meantime, none of the manuals out there seem to fully fit this particular model. So I take ideas from all of them and decide what works best for me at any one time. Unless you are in the fortunate position of having found your personal, secret manual, I encourage you also to explore different ideas and to choose for yourself what works best for you.

Pay attention not only to *what* Is being said, but to *how* it is being said and how the person saying it is relating to you and trying to motivate you. An interesting thing about any group or teaching that is hard-line or dogmatic is that it is, in effect, telling you what you should do to be okay.

The subtle or not-so-subtle inference is that if you don't do it *their way* then you should be afraid – be very, very afraid! In the name of empowering you, it appeals to your need to feel safe and certain, to belong to the club and to be accepted by it. This can stop you from accessing your own wisdom and understanding. In my training classes for coaches, I am glad when someone feels safe enough to disagree openly with something. It means that I am creating an environment where participants are thinking for themselves.

My approach to needs

My approach to working with needs is based on telling the truth about what really does and does not work for you. I emphasize taking responsibility for how you deal with what you need, including how you do or do not involve other people. I also find it important to look at needs from within the larger context of what it takes for you to be happy, living your life to the full and making your unique contribution to the world. Focusing on getting what you need, without this bigger positive context, can become obsessive, dreary and never-ending.

When you recognize that you are being driven or affected by an unmet need then there are two complementary approaches you can take. The first is to change your attitude so as to be genuinely happy without the need and the second is to do what you can to get the need met. A joint approach is often most effective.

The first approach can be thought of as being happy when *you choose to want what you've got*. The second can be thought of as being happy when *you do what you can to get what you want*. In theory, the more you can be happy with whatever you've got, the freer you are. In practice, most of us have certain needs that, if met, make it a lot *easier* to be happy.

If you take every preference and treat it as an essential need then you will make life hard for yourself and will be difficult to be around. On the other hand, if you ignore or deny your needs, or pretend to be fine when you are not, then you will be unhappy, less resourceful, and less effective. And, once again, you will be difficult to be around.

The one extreme is illustrated by the story of a king who told his servants to cover his kingdom in leather, so that he wouldn't hurt his feet as he walked around. His wise adviser suggested that if the king were to wear shoes then he could still protect his feet and could happily go to more places and do more things! The other extreme would be like having rocks all over your lawn and your living-room carpet and boulders blocking the door. You *could* exist with them but life would be a lot more pleasant if you were to clear the rocks and could walk barefoot sometimes ….

So take an honest look at what does and does not work for you, what is important to you and how you can go about making things better. You get to say whether any particular need is an essential requirement, or highly desirable or useful but not that big a deal – for *you*. For somebody else it may be different.

Reflection point *Acceptance or denial*

Where are you on the spectrum between, on the one hand, turning every wish into an essential need and, on the other hand, being in denial of your needs?

Where would you benefit from learning to accept, and be happier with, the way things already are?

Where would you benefit from clearing away some rocks and getting your needs met?

Getting your needs met

Consider yourself to be:

- An organic, physical entity needing nourishment and maintenance
- A feeling, interactive, social person
- A cognitive, thinking person
- An aesthetic, creative and expressive individual
- A spiritual being

All of these interweave in the entirety of who and what you are. Body, emotions, mind and spirit are different aspects of your whole self and, while a role or activity may emphasize one aspect more than another, they are all involved in and affected by everything you do. When you have a cold or are physically run down, you are likely to be emotionally more sensitive and your thinking may not be as clear. Conversely, if you are worried and stressed then you are more likely to get ill and to take longer to recover. When you are spiritually nourished, it affects your whole health and well-being. And if you are deeply in love then your whole demeanour and presence in the world are transformed. That said, it can still be helpful to consider the different aspects of your being, one by one.

We are now going to look at each area in some depth. Later in the chapter, you will find the Needs Review, which is a self-assessment of how well your different needs are being met. If you prefer, you can take the assessment first and then go to whichever sections are most relevant for you.

Physical Needs

Your body is the vehicle through which you experience life and express yourself. As well as having a reverence for the gift that you have been given, it makes good common sense to take care of it as well as you can, particularly as life-expectancy has increased dramatically in recent decades.

Physical maintenance

Many people hesitate to give themselves a fraction of the time for physical renewal and ongoing maintenance that they would devote to their car or the company photocopier. When I worked as an Alexander teacher, I supported clients in living in a more body-friendly way. I would often ask them to spend 20 minutes per day lying down, consciously allowing their body to release tension and realign itself. Many clients felt guilty about putting aside this much time for themselves. Yet if they fell ill or needed to visit a doctor or chiropractor, as a result of not taking good care of themselves, then everyone had to get on without them for a much greater period of time in the long run. The difference was that the illness 'happened to them' whereas they would have to choose, and take responsibility for, looking after themselves. The costs of continually not taking care of your physical needs − including diet, rest and exercise − are enormous for your own well-being, for your ability to function well when needed, and for the example you model for your children.

CASE STUDY ~ ALISON

Alison was an area manager overseeing a group of charity shops. She would rush between shops, take minimum lunch breaks and work flat out at each shop, always finding more to do whether it was necessary or not. Then she would go home and look after her two children. She felt continually stressed and suffered from neck and back tension. As we discussed her situation, she realized that, not only was she feeling very stressed, but that this way of doing things was leaving her less effective at work than she could be. She agreed to take regular lunch breaks away from the shops and to walk calmly rather than racing everywhere. She also agreed to stop for a break between shops so that she could peacefully review what she had been doing and prepare for what she would do next. After a week she felt much more relaxed and found that she was still doing everything that needed doing. After two weeks she reported that she felt so relaxed and work felt so much easier that she found herself giggling to herself, with a kind of disbelief that she could feel so good and still get paid! When we talked about it, she realized that she had bought into a common belief that if you are not stressed and suffering then you're not working properly!

This same belief is illustrated in a story told to me by Marjory Barlow, the niece of F. M. Alexander who was the founder of the Alexander Technique. Marjory and her husband, Dr Wilfred Barlow, were themselves highly respected teachers of the technique and I was lucky enough to have weekly lessons with Marjory for almost two years. Their son came home from boarding school at the end of one term distressed by his report card, which said that he needed to try harder. 'What do they want?' he asked, 'I'm top of the class!' The 'problem' was that, given the role models of his parents, he was naturally poised and physically relaxed; he didn't demonstrate the symptoms of stress and physical tension that this teacher expected to see in someone who was 'trying hard enough'. Thankfully, his parents were able to reassure him and encourage him to carry on doing what he was doing. How many of us have learned to associate stress and struggle with doing a good job, to such an extent that when we don't feel stressed we feel guilty that we are not working hard enough?

Amongst the physical needs that you may want to consider meeting more fully and healthily are: rest and renewal; diet; exercise; having home and work environments that nourish and inspire you; and your needs for touch and sexuality.

Doing it your way

If you want to relax more then you may find yoga or meditation useful. Then again, you might prefer to go fishing, take your time cooking a nice meal, have a quiet drink with a friend or whatever else works for you. Jogging or going down the gym might be the right exercise for you or perhaps you would prefer to put your golden oldies on the stereo and bop around the living room. Yet again, doing the housework energetically and walking rather than using the car might fit the bill. Some people like to start the day with some kind of exercise routine while my own preference is to start writing earlier in the morning and to schedule a long lunch break when I can take a walk in nature. The bottom line is to recognize the need and then to find the ways of satisfying it that work best for you and which you can maintain.

You can consult different books or professionals to get further ideas. You may also want to get the support of a friend or a group such as a weight-loss club, an exercise group or a meditation or relaxation class. You can deal with some of these activities on your own while others may involve negotiation with the different people in your life. If you have a good idea of what you would like to do but keep putting it off, take a look at the section on procrastination in chapter 7.

Reflection point   *Taking care of your physical needs*

Think of one of your physical needs that you have been neglecting.

What difference would it make to you and others if you took better care of it?

What are the implications if you continue not to take care of it?

What would be involved in getting this need met?

What steps could you take this week to improve things?

What support do you need to make a sustainable change?

Emotional and relatedness needs

You don't live in a vacuum. A great relationship with yourself goes hand in hand with the ability to enjoy healthy, interdependent relationships where physical and emotional needs are met and where you also feel yourself contributing to the well-being of other people. Relationships require regular quality time, communication and renewal if they are to flourish. This is true at work as well as in your personal life. One of the most exciting developments in business and education, in recent years, has been the recognition and promotion of emotional intelligence.

Amongst the relatedness needs that you may want to get met more fully and healthily are: companionship; fun and recreation; listening and understanding; appreciation and respect; and contributing to others.

Particularly with the different emotional needs, there is always a balance between how much you give to yourself and how much you expect to get from other people. If you don't befriend, listen to, appreciate and support yourself then what kind of message are you giving out to other people? If you don't value yourself enough to bother then why should they? In the next chapter, about empowering yourself, there are ideas and tools for how you can give yourself this kind of support.

The main focus of this book is on the relationship with yourself, which provides the foundation for good relationships with other people. At the same time, for most of us, the truth is that even when we take good care of ourselves, it also makes one heck of a difference who our friends, companions and colleagues are, and how they treat us.

So start with giving yourself what you ideally want from others and with treating yourself and them as you like to be treated ... AND ... where possible choose friends and relationships that nourish you ... AND ... be willing to communicate your needs, set boundaries and make requests.

Communicating in relationships

No matter how well-intentioned the people in your life are, they are not usually mind readers. Clear communication is the foundation stone on which good, nourishing relationships are built.

CASE STUDY ~ BRENDA & JERRY

Brenda worked in a restaurant and felt very unhappy with the way her boss would sometimes correct her in front of more junior staff. Brenda had been putting up with this for two years when she shared her frustration and upset in an ongoing coaching group. When people are unhappy with any situation, I usually take a two-pronged approach of exploring possible alternatives while at the same time doing whatever you can to make the present situation better. If you are on the point of leaving somewhere anyway, then you can afford to take some risks and to learn what you can where you are. Simply complaining about how things were was keeping Brenda stuck so, after allowing her a little time to vent her frustrations, I coached her to take responsibility for what she needed. She agreed to simultaneously explore other opportunities and to have a conversation with her present boss. She found another job possibility and then spoke with her boss and told her that she was thinking of leaving. Her boss was upset as she actually really valued Brenda. They had a good heart to heart where the boss also expressed some of her difficulties and what she needed from Brenda. Brenda now really loves her job again, and also knows that if that changes then she can choose to move on.

In the same coaching group, Jerry was a supervisor in an electrical engineering firm. He felt unappreciated by his boss and frequently disrespected by his team. Jerry explored the possibilities of setting up a taxi business and applied for a licence with the local authority. With the support of the group, he also arranged a meeting with his boss and told him how he felt about things. His boss was more than supportive, told Jerry how much he did appreciate him and moved him to a different team who were much easier to work with. Jerry is still looking to set up his own business at some point, but in the meantime his needs for appreciation and respect are being met and he enjoys going into work again.

Notice that both Brenda and Jerry had to take responsibility for their needs and respect themselves enough to ask for respect from other people. Also, if things didn't change then they were ready to look at alternatives.

From complaining to making requests

As an adult, you are responsible for recognising and dealing with your own needs and you cannot off-load that responsibility onto other people or make it their job to make you happy. What you can do is to choose to hang around with people who generally help you feel good and be willing to make requests for how you would like to be treated. If they don't want to cooperate, then either you accept that and find other ways of meeting your needs or else you choose to leave the situation or the person.

What doesn't work is to spend large chunks of time complaining to or about other people. You don't have to be a saint and a certain amount of venting and letting off steam is human and understandable and can be therapeutic. Clearing the air and expressing your feelings can sometimes prepare the ground for deciding how you are going to handle things. But if you use complaining as a way of life then it is disempowering and draining, both for you and for the people who listen to you. And if you are part of a group of people who spend a lot of time complaining then you're in your own little victims' club. You can pretend to yourself, and to each other, that by complaining about somebody or something you've actually done something useful; in reality, it's usually a way of giving away your power and putting up with things.

This is especially relevant to close relationships. Do what you can to get your needs met, including making requests of the other person, and then choose to stay or to leave. If, however, you spend a lot of time complaining that *they* don't treat you right or that *they* make you feel bad, rather than asking for what it is that you *do* want, then maybe it's time to grow up and to take a little more responsibility.

Often, when you ask a habitual complainer what it is that they *do* want, they can't tell you. Yet the implication is that other people should be mind-readers and know for them. They act as if they are small children surrounded by adults whose job it is to know what they need and to give it to them. If you are not ready to do the work to find out what it is that you do really want and need then don't expect other people to do it for you. They have their own needs and happiness to take care of.

Reflection point   **From complaining to requests**

Where are your needs not being met with other people?

Do you complain and blame – or do you clarify what you would like and make requests?

Who do you need to have a conversation with?

Boundaries

If you let people do whatever they want around you, or passively go along with whatever they want, then you become a doormat. And people with footprints on their face don't tend to look that attractive or get a huge amount of respect! If you're unable to say 'no' to people, when appropriate, then your 'yes' doesn't have much value. Only when you're able to say 'no' can you say 'yes' wholeheartedly. So it is important, if you are to get more of what you need, that you are able to state and maintain healthy boundaries.

You need boundaries:

- To protect yourself and your life
- To choose how you use your time and energy
- To allow yourself to interact and contribute healthily

When setting boundaries:

- Focus on what works for you – don't put others in the wrong

- Make the person right – address the behaviour
- Speak calmly and assertively

Four Step Boundary Model:

- Inform the person of what doesn't work for you
- Request them to change their behaviour in this regard
- State the consequences of their continuing in this behaviour
- Carry out the consequences

The heart of this approach is moving from complaining about what you don't like to making requests for what you do or would like. It is not about putting the other person in the wrong in any way.

As an example, suppose you have a friend who frequently turns up late when you arrange to meet in town somewhere. You find yourself getting uptight, resentful and/or concerned that you may have got the time wrong or that something has happened to your friend. By the time she does arrive, you wish you had never agreed to go out in the first place! You don't actually say anything to her but instead are grumpy and punish her with a little coolness for the next hour. You actually really like her, so, about an hour or so later, you forget about the start of the evening and have a good time. Then it happens again. And then again! This time you blast her and tell her what a selfish cow she is, how bad she makes you feel and imply that she has now really got to make it up to you before she earns your precious forgiveness.

Okay, confession time – that was me and how I used to handle things. I was unable to see the distinction between how I liked things to be and how they 'ought' to be. When my friend arranged to see some of her other friends, there was no problem as they had the same attitude towards time and punctuality as she did. But it didn't work for me.

A few years later a similar scenario occurred with another friend. This time I was able to tell him that it didn't work for me when he turned up late when we arranged to meet out somewhere. I asked him if he was willing to commit to being on time. He wasn't ready to go along with this so I said that, in that case, if he wanted to go out with me then he would have to pick me up at my place first. He agreed and that's how we set things up from then on. It wasn't about who was right or wrong: it was about what was going to work for us both.

If you use this model, it is very important that you don't state consequences unless you're prepared to carry them out; otherwise you just back yourself into a corner. In some circumstances, it may work better for you to have the consequences in mind but not to state them immediately. For instance, you may decide to leave your job if your requests for improvements at work are not taken on board. When the time is right and you have a new job lined up, then you hand in your notice. Threatening to leave when you're not in a position to carry it out may not work well. Then again, it may be what is needed to bring about a change. There are no hard and fast rules.

If you find it difficult to stand up for yourself generally, start with treating yourself as well as you can and, at the same time, gradually develop your ability to speak out more. You may find that a book or a course on assertiveness will help you, as well as getting the support of a friend or a coach or mentor of some kind.

Dealing with past needs

Alongside the present day emotional needs, most of us carry leftovers from the past that get tangled up and confused with them. If you felt deprived of something in your childhood, it can continue to nag away in the background when you are an adult. For instance, if one or both of your parents never praised you as a child, then as an adult you may be attracted to partners and bosses who don't praise and appreciate you openly and, even when you are praised, you may have trouble letting it in.

If the feelings connected with a particular unmet need are overwhelming then it can be very helpful to work with a good therapist or counsellor.

Here, we'll consider some possibilities for dealing with those nagging needs that, while you can live with them without losing the plot, can seem to drive you and dominate your life year after year. Tell-tale signs are when you feel miserable, churlish, resentful or are otherwise reacting in a childish way – i.e. that you yourself feel is out of proportion to the situation. The little kid in you is acting out and, despite promises to yourself, you don't seem to be very effective at getting him or her to see sense! You've tried ignoring them, threatening them and disowning them, all with limited success. Not only that, but you seem to attract into your life the kind of people and situations that make it worse. Out in the world, you may become reasonably adept at covering it all up but when you're with the people that you feel really close to and love the most, that's when the old pattern really rears its ugly head. It is usually my partner who gets to experience Duncan, aged fifty-plus going on three-and-a-half!

When dealing with unmet needs, here are some factors to consider:

- Accept responsibility for dealing with your needs now
- Recognize the symptoms pointing to unmet needs
- Release any judgement of yourself for feeling needy
- Recognize and name the need that is driving you
- Acknowledge and shift any beliefs that are associated with the need
- Find new and creative ways of meeting the need in present time

These apply to any unmet need and are particularly helpful to consider when dealing with troublesome, unmet needs from the past.

If you find yourself edgy, resentful, beaten down, depressed, cantankerous, belligerent, tearful or in some other emotional upset, then it's likely that you are not getting something that you need. This could be safety, enough rest, a better diet, companionship, recognition, positive inspiration, meaning or any number of other things.

Reflection point   **Symptoms of unmet needs**

What symptoms do you display when your needs are not being met?

What particular unmet need do these symptoms point to?

Judging yourself for feeling off form doesn't help. If you judge yourself, you are likely to try to suppress the feelings or otherwise try and bully yourself into feeling better. Neither approach is likely to work well in the long-term. Accepting yourself, feeling the way you do, gives you the possibility of doing something about it. Notice what seems to trigger you and ask yourself what it is that you seem to need more of. Tell the truth to yourself even if you can't see how to get it. You can look at the Needs Review later in the chapter to get some ideas of different needs that may be involved.

It may be that, once you have acknowledged it, you can now see your way clear to getting the need met. On the other hand, particularly if this is an old, established pattern, you may have developed some limiting beliefs around what is possible for you and what you can have.

Let's consider the example of not being praised enough when you were a child. Symptoms of this may include finding yourself over-dependent on praise from others and feeling mortified if you are criticized. Inwardly you may feel like a little doggy ready to sit up and wag your tail for a morsel of praise, even though you hate yourself for acting this way. Or else you may have gone the opposite way, in an attempt to escape the yucky feelings, and now make a point of aggressively letting everybody know that you don't care what anybody thinks! You may even feel angry in some way and feel belittled or patronized if somebody does praise you. Either way you are being driven by the unmet need. Promise.

On top of the original hurt that went with not being praised you probably learned, at some point, to judge yourself for being needy. You may also have developed limiting beliefs along the lines of, 'the reason I am never praised is because there is something wrong with me and I don't deserve it' or, 'I can only be praised if I'm perfect'.

As a child, with limited perspective, that was probably the best reason you could come up with to make sense of why someone would withhold their approval from you. You didn't understand that the adults in your life had their own problems and limitations, which weren't your fault. I'm not knocking your parents here and I'm not making them responsible for what you do and how you feel NOW. I'm simply wanting you to understand and have a little compassion for yourself; at the same time that I'm encouraging you to take full responsibility for dealing with things. Blaming your parents for what they did, and for what beliefs they may have instilled in you, gets in the way of your choosing what to do and what to believe from now on.

We touched on beliefs in the last chapter and you'll find more on them in the next chapter, about empowering yourself. For now, a helpful question to ask yourself is:

> 'What would I need to believe about myself so that it would feel comfortable and natural for me to get this need met?'

CASE STUDY ~ KARINA

Karina was a participant in one of my group coaching sessions. She was a very talented jazz singer touring in the US. Despite getting good reviews and feedback, she lacked confidence in herself and was holding herself back from developing her career. When anyone said anything positive to her she deflected it with some self-depreciating remark, even though it was clear that she had a deep need for appreciation. Her underlying belief was, 'Only when I'm perfect and have reached the top will I deserve praise'. As a result she denied herself the positive encouragement that she yearned for and which she needed in order to move forward. As we explored together, she found that a more freeing belief for her was, 'I'm good enough to be appreciated and to be successful now'. To get her used to receiving praise, I asked her to stand up and extend her arms to the side so that her heart area was open. Then the rest of the group took turns to give her positive feedback. After each person spoke, Karina simply had to say, 'Thank you for noticing that; I appreciate it.' At the end she was beaming. The ongoing fieldwork was, firstly, to continue saying this to herself every time she was praised and, secondly, to encourage herself with praise rather than with criticism. Two weeks later, she reported back that not only was she feeling brilliant but she had also accepted a new booking, which was a step up in her career.

Reflection point   Unmet needs from the past

What unmet need from the past is still causing you problems in the present?

What would you need to believe about yourself so that it would feel comfortable and natural for you to get this need met now?

*How can you **now** start to get this need met more healthily?*

Cognitive and thinking needs

You are a cognitive thinking being and, as such, you need mental stimulation and to find meaning in situations and in life generally. Amongst the mental needs that you may want to meet more fully and healthily are: stimulation from conversation and media; curiosity and learning; problem solving; planning; control and order.

Our intellectual needs are more recognized and accepted in society generally, which can make it easier for them to be expressed and taken care of.

Thinking or recycling?

However, a lot of what people call thinking actually consists of recycling the same old ideas and thoughts that have either been fed to them or that they adopted at some time in their past. You can be reading through this, or any other book, and simply checking it off against what you are already familiar with; anything that fits gets a mental tick of approval and anything that doesn't is ignored. And yet, if you keep thinking and doing what you have always thought and done then you will keep getting what you have always got. Real thinking takes some time and reflection and a willingness to live with and explore an idea. That is why I put in the reflection points and ask you questions to help you think more deeply about what is or might be true for you.

This section is not so much written as dictated as I am walking near my home in the grounds of a local castle. There's a long avenue of trees with a grass thoroughfare leading to a lake, with swans, at the end of it. This is my daily walk scheduled around lunchtime. It's been snowing and I know it's extra cold today because I'm having to use my gloves to operate my digital recorder, which is a bit tricky as it is quite small and trying to press the buttons with a glove on is not easy. There is something about being away from the desk and the computer screen that supplements the work that I do there, where I am being structured and ordered. As I walk here new thoughts come, or else variations on the thoughts that I have already explored. They come in their own rhythm, timing and sequence and seem to inform the structure, as well as frequently forming the basis, for what I get to write about next.

Away from the screen or the written page, I mull over the ideas. Some thoughts germinate and blossom and others fall away. In the same way, you will get most from this book if you allow yourself to live with the ideas for a while. Explore them, chew them over and, if necessary, spit them out before swallowing something and making it yours.

Are your cognitive and thinking needs being met?

People's circumstances and individual needs vary considerably and only you can say whether your mental needs are being met satisfactorily. You may need to develop some new contacts with whom you can explore and express ideas freely. You may need to buy another TV or grab the remote control more quickly before yet another reality TV show liquefies your brain. If your work doesn't give you the mental stimulation you need then you can look for alternatives or else join the ranks of the thousands of people going through home-study courses.

Reflection point **Mental and Intellectual needs**

How fully are your mental and intellectual needs being met?

What, if anything, would lead to your being more satisfied in this area?

Aesthetic, creative and expressive needs

Included here are the needs for beauty, appreciation of the arts, creating things and ideas, self-expression and performance, and a sense of making a meaningful difference in the world.

As well as mental stimulation, different people need different kinds of aesthetic inspiration, whether it comes from the beauty of their environment or from quality music and art. A really good movie can be food for the soul as well as for the mind.

You are also unique with your own talents, gifts and perspective. For life to be meaningful you need to find ways of honouring and expressing your individuality and creativity in the world and you need environments and people that support this.

Reflection
point **Aesthetic and creative needs**

How much do you enjoy and express your aesthetic and creative sides?

What do you need to let you expand this in the different areas of your life?

In the sphere of creativity, people often hold themselves back by comparing their efforts to those of established professionals and by not allowing themselves to simply enjoy expressing themselves and their creativity in different areas. You do not have to be a Robbie Williams or a Placido Domingo to enjoy singing. And you can enjoy writing, sketching or painting just because you do.

Your expression of creativity might be cooking and serving a meal that tastes and looks beautiful or it might be working in your garden. Then again, you might express your creativity at work by coming up with new ways of doing things. Creativity is a reward in itself and does not have to be connected with fame and recognition – even though it might be for some people whose careers are in these areas.

Creativity and expression are part of our human nature. Just watch young children and see how readily and naturally they play, create and perform. Later they learn to judge themselves and to limit what they will allow themselves to do.

> ### *Reflection point*   **What did you enjoy as a child?**
>
> *What did you love to do when you were a young child?*
>
> *How much do you do that now?*
>
> *How could you start to bring more of that into your life?*

An excellent book for helping you to re-connect with and express your creativity is *The Artist's Way* by Julia Cameron (Pan Books, 1995). When I worked through it, rather than thinking of a particular 'artistic' expression, I held the intention of making my life more of a work of art. In the same way, you get to exercise your creativity every time that you adapt ideas or methods to make them work for you.

When considering some of the 'higher level' needs, you'll find that they can cross over into what are sometimes called values, which are explored more fully in the chapter on listening to yourself.

Spiritual needs

Amongst the spiritual needs that you may want to consider are: inspiration; meaning and purpose; quiet connecting time; time in nature; gratitude and celebration; and practising kindness and generosity of spirit.

Religion and spirituality

If you have a particular religion or path that you adhere to then that can be a great source of comfort as well as providing you with a community and structures for connecting with and expressing your spiritual self. I have clients who belong to various traditional religions as well as ones who take a more New Age approach. I also have clients, whom I would consider to be deeply spiritual in how they live their lives and treat other people, who don't follow any particular approach or even see themselves as spiritual.

For me, spirituality is about having a sense and appreciation of the underlying mystery of life and a quality of connection to a deeper source of strength and wisdom than that which comes from just thinking and logic alone. It is also about how you treat others and about how you are being in the moment. If the person behind the till at the local supermarket notices that an old lady is struggling to find her change – and re-assures her and helps her then I see that as an expression of spirituality. If, in the name of religion, I see intolerance and hatred then I figure that they have lost the plot and are disconnected from their spiritual source. The Dalai Lama, who is one of the most universally-respected religious figures, often says that the basis of Buddhism, as of most religions, is kindness.

One common paradigm views humans as physical beings endeavouring to become spiritual. Another way of seeing things is that we are spiritual beings experiencing, and learning from, being in a physical body and environment. Our essential self as loving, spontaneous, joyful and expressive cannot be lost but it can be forgotten. Many of our modern crises of meaning are a result of becoming disconnected from our essential nature. Different folk have different ways of supporting their being connected. These include prayer and meditation as well as quiet time alone, being in nature, singing, dancing and music, fishing, gardening and much more. What supports you in connecting with your spiritual source and do you make enough time for it?

Reflection point   **Connecting with your spiritual source**

How do you best connect with your spiritual source?

What can you do on a weekly basis to be more spiritually nourished?

*What can you do on a daily basis, or as you go about your day,
to help you keep in touch with your spiritual source?*

What changes will you choose to make this week?

Who, or what, will support you in this?

Your needs and other people

You don't live in isolation and we have looked a little at meeting your
emotional needs in relation to other people. Even when others are not
directly involved in meeting your needs, they will be affected by your
decisions, particularly around how you will prioritize and use your time.
Some negotiation will be needed and you may also need to communicate
and enforce boundaries about what you are and are not okay with other
people doing. Depending on your circumstances, there may be some real
limits on what you can have and do for yourself. Even so, most of my
clients find that they can take far more responsibility for their needs and
do much more for themselves than they have done previously. The
writings of all major religions contain their own version of the Christian
dictum: 'Do unto others as you would have done unto yourself'. Note
that this doesn't ask you to sacrifice yourself, or treat others better, but
to treat others *as you yourself would like to be treated*. If you take poor
care of yourself, then what are the implications for what you will expect
of, and how you will treat, others?

*Reflection
point*   **How to treat yourself in relation to others**

*Think of a child or loved one and ask yourself how you would ideally
like to see them being treated. Is this how you treat yourself?*

*Children and others learn most by imitation. Does the way that you
take care of yourself, and get your needs met, provide them with a
good role model?*

I am not a great fan of unnecessary sacrifice because of the resentful
background feelings that tend to go with it. There are some situations
with children, and vulnerable dependent others, where their needs will
have to come first and life is not always a bed of roses. However, in the
long term, you do yourself and everyone else a favour if you take
responsibility for getting your needs met as fully as is possible.

Sacrifice comes at a cost and the people you 'make sacrifices for' often
pay for it with guilt or some other emotional manipulation. As an ex-
partner of mine used to say: 'Duncan, don't try too hard to be nice
because I will always pay for it in the end!' By this she didn't mean don't
be nice or loving; it was when I was 'trying to be nice' that she learned
to watch her back!

I have worked with many clients, helping them to meet their needs while
living well with other people. I don't suggest walking over or taking
advantage of your friends, colleagues or family. It isn't a case of either
you or them: it's about both you *and* them. I encourage you to help the
other people in your life to express and get their needs met, too. Create
the space and the possibility for them and you to express your needs.
This doesn't mean that people always have to do what you want any
more than you always have to do what they want. Taking responsibility
for getting your needs met includes asking other people to assist you
and accepting that they won't always want to.

Some people recommend that you meet all your needs yourself and
don't rely on anyone else as this just results in your being needy and

disempowered. Certainly if you try to force or manipulate people into giving you what you want, even when they don't want to, then you are not going to be fun to be around and this is not going to help your relationships. To avoid this some people deny that they have unmet needs and become stoically self-reliant and rigid in their bodies and their attitudes. Once again, they are not so much fun to be around! Tricky, ay? And, if you only rely on yourself and you have a bad day or a bad week, then where is the back up?

The bottom line is that you, and nobody else, is responsible for taking care of yourself and seeing that you get what you need to be happy, to function well and to be in a generally resourceful state. Part of how you do that will involve making requests of, or negotiating with, other people. In fact, being needy in relationships is often a result of denying your needs and not asking for what you need in an open, respectful and adult way.

Of course, if you rely solely on your partner for all your needs, this can put a strain on them and on your relationship. It's healthiest to get your needs met from a variety of sources. These include:

- Yourself
- Your partner
- Your family
- Your friends
- Your colleagues
- Particular groups
- Paid professionals

For couples

The main focus of this book is on the relationship that you develop with yourself, as the basis for good relationships with others, and we are just touching on your external relationships in this section. The more that you take care of and empower yourself, the more you will be able to develop interdependent, synergistic relationships.

Particularly in intimate relationships, it is very easy to slip into blame or to try and invalidate each other's position rather than acknowledging each other's concerns and seeing if you can come up with a solution that serves you both.

Most intimate relationships will benefit from more frequent and clearer communication. Here is a simple, yet profound exercise that a number of couples have found helpful when dealing with an issue or talking about each other's needs.

Couples exercise

Start sitting on opposite sides of a table and take it in turns to speak for 5-10 minutes and to express your concerns, needs and wishes. When your partner is speaking, simply listen. At the end, feed back to them what you have heard and list their different concerns and wishes, as you understood them. They can then say whether or not that matches with what they felt they said. If necessary, ask them questions and clarify things until you are able to represent their point of view clearly. You do not have to agree with them but you do need to accept that their concerns are valid and be ready to state them as such. When they feel that you have understood their different concerns and wishes then write them down on a piece of paper. Then swap over and have your partner do the same with you until your concerns and wishes are also listed on the paper. Now move your seats and sit side-by-side, as a team, with the combined list of concerns and wishes in front of you both. Now explore, together, possible ways of taking care of them, as if they belonged to you both.

Reflection point   **You and close relationships**

Do you give enough time to your important relationships?

Do you express your needs and boundaries in relationship and are you able to listen to and validate the needs of others and negotiate a healthy balance?

What have you been avoiding that needs to be spoken about?

Apples and oranges for couples

As we said earlier, our old unmet needs are most likely to surface in intimate relationships. If you can find a way of working together on this, there is a great opportunity for healing and growth. One very common misunderstanding is that in order to show love all we need to do is to give our partner the same things that we like to get. Big mistake!

Too often the trouble is that, metaphorically, you like oranges and they like apples. So you give them a nice big Jaffa orange knowing that, if only they would give you one of these juicy delights, you would be ecstatic – your very heart would thrill and you would embrace them with love and tenderness. But they are unmoved! They do not even peel the orange; in fact they look disappointed. So you sulk for a few days in a very meaningful and adult way, alternating between glowering at them and giving them your special hurt look with the big sad eyes. However you're a big chap and seeing as you do really love her you try again. This time you buy her some lovely tangerines and say nothing when three days later they are still untouched in the fruit bowl. What's wrong with this miserable bitch, anyway? you grumble. Then, in a moment of relief you realise what the problem might be – maybe she prefers satsumas … .

Meanwhile, you hardly notice the apples that she has been buying and leaving for you. First it was Cox's Orange Pippins, a lovely crisp apple she has always thought. Who could possibly not appreciate them? She's also tried Granny Smith's, Golden Delicious and those other red ones that you don't even know the name of.

Maybe it's time for the two of you to have a good fruit to fruit talk.

Time to tell each other what the other one can give you that really makes you feel loved, appreciated and special. In telling them what they can do for you, be as specific as you can. And give them a lot of options to choose from. Some people balk at this exercise and say that if you have to tell someone what they can give you then it doesn't count – they should do it spontaneously. I don't buy into this way of thinking. To me it's infantile and connected with the idea that when you were a baby your parents had to guess what you wanted because you couldn't speak. But take a look in the mirror and you may notice that some changes have taken place. You're supposed to be a grown-up now, so open your mouth and speak! Think of it from another perspective. If somebody is just doing what they happen to like doing then it is not such a big deal. Somebody's bothering to listen to you and being willing to do what YOU would like is a real demonstration of caring and love. You can keep a sense of spontaneity around it by giving them lots of options to choose from. For many men, particularly, the generalized complaint that they are not loving enough fills them with dread because they haven't got a clue what to do about it. When they are given some specific instructions or requests the sense of relief can be palpable!

The above approaches have been useful for many couples and they may or may not work for you. Keep communicating and keep exploring together until you find a way of dealing with things that works for both of you.

There are many helpful books and resources on communicating better in close relationships. In the UK, the Relate organization publishes a number of excellent books as well as providing counselling for couples.

Families and needs

Getting your needs met when you have children can be a particular challenge, especially for women. Women are often conditioned to believe and to feel that anything they give to themselves is at the expense of what they ought to give to their children and their family. When speaking about this, with my clients and with the coaches I train, the general consensus is that, while men and women can both feel this way and need support, it is particularly challenging for women. In addition, women who are single parents or who go out to work can easily fall into the trap of trying to make up for things to their children by sacrificing themselves and their own well-being.

The reality is that when you have children you do agree to take care of their needs. While you reap the many benefits and joys of being a parent, you also have to accept some limitations on what you can then do. It's all part of the deal. However, many parents unnecessarily sacrifice their own well-being to such an extent that not only do *they* suffer but so do their families. Children end up with a parent who is stressed out, snappy and nowhere near as resourceful and as much fun as they could be. So in the end, everybody pays the price.

Also, children learn most by imitation. Is the way that you take care of yourself now the way that you would like them to take care of themselves when they are older? Do you want your daughter to act this way when she's a mother? Do you want your son to grow up expecting that his future wife or partner will do what you do? And, if you don't take time for yourself, what message does it give about how you value and respect yourself? If you don't demonstrate that you value and respect yourself then why should your children value and respect you?

The needs that take time are the ones that are most often ignored or pushed aside. These include relaxation, exercise, alone time and quality time with other adults. It can help you to give a higher priority to some of these needs if you realize that multiple benefits, with positive indications for everybody, are being met by the same activity.

The five benefits, to yourself and to others, of meeting your needs:

- You get the direct benefits of self-care and support
- You give yourself the message that you matter and are valued
- You are in a more resourceful state – they get a better you
- They learn to include another's needs and to work as a team
- You model for them that it is good to appreciate and take care of themselves

When you realize this, it can help you escape from the all-or-nothing mentality. Supposing that you would ideally like to put aside an hour for your exercise routine and that more than 30 minutes is going to be really difficult. You may be tempted to forget it all together. But if you set things up to do 30 minutes of exercise then you get some direct benefit from the exercise, together with all the other benefits listed above. So accept that there are some limitations AND still do what you can to take care of your needs.

CASE STUDY ~ MARY

Mary was a freelance journalist who was training as a coach and had a baby boy of 18 months. She had previously enjoyed competitive running and had put off getting back into running because she would no longer be able to give the time it took to compete. She finally went along for a run at her local club and found how much the companionship and support gave her, without necessarily having to compete. She now goes to the club twice a week and her husband is more than willing to support her in this – not only is he a runner himself but he appreciates that having Mary fitter and happier benefits the whole family.

We have looked together at your needs, in relation to the different aspects of yourself. Now we can put them together and get an overview of how well you are getting your needs met, and where you may want to give more attention and higher priority.

The Needs Review

Use the Needs Review on the opposite page as a starting point for assessing your own situation. If you don't agree with something there, or feel that something is left out, then adjust it so that it works best for you.

When you have completed the Needs Review, choose two or three needs that you would like to meet more fully. For each one, ask yourself the following questions and write down your replies:

- How do I feel when this need is not being met?
- How do I feel when this need *is* being met?
- What difference would it make if I took better care of this need?
- What are the implications if I continue *not* to take care of it?
- What would be involved in getting this need met more fully?
- How would I like things to be in three months' time, and that is achievable?
- What steps can I take this week to start to improve things?
- What support do I need in order to make this a sustainable change?

Now start to make changes. Remember that the journey of a thousand miles begins with the first step. So take your first steps now, whether they are baby ones or huge strides ... .

Energy maintenance

Another complementary way of looking at your personal sustainability is in terms of your own, natural, renewable energy system. For this to be

Needs Review

Score each item out of 4, according to how far you feel that need is currently being met in your life. Be honest about how you feel about it and don't compare yourself to how you think it 'should' be.

Physical Needs	Rest & Relaxation ⎯⎯	Diet ⎯⎯
	Exercise ⎯⎯	Healthy Environment ⎯⎯
	Touch & Sexuality ⎯⎯	**Total** ⎯⎯ **/ 20**
Emotional & Relatedness Needs	Companionship ⎯⎯	Fun and Recreation ⎯⎯
	Listening & Understanding ⎯⎯	Appreciation & Respect ⎯⎯
	Contributing to Others ⎯⎯	**Total** ⎯⎯ **/ 20**
Cognitive & Mental Needs	Stimulating Conversation ⎯⎯	Stimulating Reading/ TV/Movies ⎯⎯
	Problem Solving ⎯⎯	Exercising Curiosity/ Learning new things ⎯⎯
	Planning, Control & Order ⎯⎯	**Total** ⎯⎯ **/ 20**
Aesthetic, Creative & Expressive Needs	Beauty in Environment ⎯⎯	Appreciating Art/Music/ Theatre ⎯⎯
	Creating Things and/or Ideas ⎯⎯	Self-Expression/ Performance ⎯⎯
	Making a Difference in the World ⎯⎯	**Total** ⎯⎯ **/ 20**
Spiritual Needs	Gratitude / Celebration ⎯⎯	Prayer/Meditation/ Quiet Connecting Time ⎯⎯
	Time in Nature ⎯⎯	Inspiration, Meaning & Purpose ⎯⎯
	Practising Kindness & Generosity of Spirit ⎯⎯	**Total** ⎯⎯ **/ 20**
	Grand Total	⎯⎯ **/ 100**

sustainable, your energy sources need to supply more than your energy output requires. On the one hand, you require regular inputs of energy from good healthy sources that keep you topped up and ready to go. On the other hand, you want to eliminate unnecessary and unproductive drains on your energy, so that your energy is used well and directed to the things that matter most to you.

The vase analogy

Imagine a vase being filled with water. Imagine, also, that the vase has a number of little holes from which water is leaking away. You are like that vase, receiving energy from different sources. When you are full and overflowing, then you will naturally pour out your surplus energy to nourish others and to make your contribution. However, the unsupportive environments, unmet needs and negative situations you put up with are the holes that drain you of energy. They deplete you and prevent you from living your life to the full.

Diagram showing energy flowing in from positive sources and being lost through unmet needs and tolerations.

By taking care of unmet needs you will already have begun to increase your sources of positive energy and to reduce negative energy drains. Now you get to look at what else you can do to boost your energy while, at the same time, noticing and eliminating the things that drain you.

Energy boosters

Some of these take major time and planning whilst others can become positive habits that are part of your daily or weekly routines.

Reflection point   *Taking time off*

Do you usually take evenings and weekends off or do you take work home?

What breaks or holidays do you need to re-charge your batteries?

What have you got scheduled ahead? Is it enough?

What other breaks will you now schedule in for yourself?

There are many positive things that you can schedule in to boost your energy, as part of your weekly routine. These include things like exercise, relaxation, meditation, reading a good book, or just having quiet time alone to reflect and be with yourself.

Many people start with good intentions for the things that they will do for themselves on an ongoing basis. Then the hustle and bustle of life takes over. Another week goes by and they have dropped all the quality activities that they had meant to do. The trouble is that they have tried to fit them in around everything else rather than starting by giving them a high priority and scheduling them in first. One approach that works is to book 'appointments' with yourself in your diary and to treat them with the same respect that you would treat appointments with other people. If you have put time aside for a quiet evening at home and another demand comes in, simply say that you have already got something booked for the evening. Then leave your answer machine on and don't take calls, anymore than you would if you had arranged to spend quality time with someone else.

Reflection point   *Quality time alone*

What quality time with yourself would you like to give higher priority to?

Book it in your diary now and treat it with the same respect as you would treat an appointment with someone else.

Another obvious source of energy is the food that you eat. How do you feel about your diet? You may eat enough to fill your stomach but how happy are you really with what you eat and how you treat yourself around food? Don't get caught up with 'being good' or 'doing the right thing'. Just tell the truth about what really works for you and gives you energy. Every year, if not every month, articles come out about the correct diet and the correct way to eat. These can be helpful guides and yet, if the experts themselves disagree, at the end of the day you are going to have to decide which experts (if any) you are going to listen to. What food really works for you and gives you the energy and vitality that you need to live your particular life?

Reflection point   **How healthy is your diet?**

How healthy do you feel your present diet is, on a scale of 1-10?

What would need to change for you to feel really good about your diet?

What changes are you willing to make in the next month?

What support do you need to make these changes?

Positive energy habits

Taking better care of yourself is not all about big projects or things that take a lot of time and have to be scheduled. There are lots of positive energy habits that you can build into your day which make a huge difference to your health, emotional mood and resourcefulness. On the opposite page are some ideas to get you started. Select some that fit for you or come up with some others of your own.

Start with five to ten habits to incorporate into your life over the next month. Avoid doing things just because you 'should'. Have this be a positive, uplifting experience and choose habits that you look forward to and which nourish you and give you energy. If a habit isn't working for you, let yourself adjust it or swap it for something else. It helps to keep a visual record where you will see it often. Make a list of the habits and

Energy habits to choose from

Physical	**Emotional & Relatedness**
Drink less tea or coffee	Smile at people
Have a brisk walk	Invite someone for tea/coffee
Go to bed by 10.30pm	Offer to help someone
No food or caffeine after 8pm	Set a boundary
5 helpings of fruit/vegetables per day	Phone a friend
Get outside for 20 minutes	Laugh out loud
Drink plenty of water	Appreciate somebody
Take a bath with essential oils	Have a hug
Walk calmly between locations	Notice what you do well
Take a proper lunch break	Send someone a card or a gift
Do some morning stretching	Listen to someone closely
Take a 20-minute catnap	Spend quality time with family
Cognitive and Mental	**Aesthetic/Creative/Expressive**
Simplify something	Look at the sky
Handle one unresolved matter	Notice the colours around you
Say 'no' to time wasters	Listen to good music
Plan the day ahead	Listen to a bird sing
Only watch good television	Draw a sketch / Write a poem
Remember to be curious	Dance freely
Tidy your desk at the end of the day	Find new ways of doing things
Finish work by 6pm	Look at the world with wonder
Solve a problem	Cook a special meal
Don't read non-essential email	Read a good book
Spend 20 minutes visioning	Make a difference somewhere
Learn something new	Add something new to this list
Spiritual	**Other**
Do a kindness and tell no-one	
Eat slowly and mindfully	
Keep a gratitude journal	
Follow your intuition	
Meditate or pray for 20 minutes	
Focus on a value for the day	
Read from an inspirational source	
Speak well of people	
Spend some time in nature	
Send positive thoughts to someone	
Ask for guidance about something	
Connect with your inner wisdom	

put a tick next to each one for every day that you carried it out. At the end of each week review your experience and, at the end of the month, see what you want to keep and what you might want to change or add.

Clearing Energy Drains

Remember the metaphor of the vase losing energy through all the holes. There are many nagging things that we tolerate and which drain us of energy. These include messy cupboards, un-filed paperwork, appliances that don't work properly, shoddy paintwork and furniture, unfinished projects, poor communication, unanswered emails, overflowing bins, unreturned phone calls, unpaid bills, poor boundaries, rudeness, noise pollution, cluttered rooms, living in a neighbourhood or doing a job you hate, etc. etc. etc! The list can go on and on. If you really take some time to think about the different areas of your life, it is not uncommon to find scores of energy drains, some minor and some major.

When thinking about this, don't get caught up in what you 'should' want or what you 'should' be okay with. Focus on what is true for you and what does or does not work for you. One person might be highly visual and flourish in a beautifully decorated home; anything less could be tolerated but is a constant frustration. Another person might be genuinely happy in a slightly scruffy apartment provided it is warm and the furniture is comfortable. If you are, or can be, genuinely happy with a situation even when it is not optimum, it does not have to drain you of energy. Energy drains occur when you do mind about something, are frustrated or complain and yet are not doing anything about it. The solution is either to choose to accept it happily or else to do what you can to change it.

Listing your energy drains

Start by making a list of ten energy drains at work and ten energy drains at home or in your personal life. Keep the list handy and keep adding to it every time that you notice something. Don't give yourself a hard time about this. You are simply raising your awareness and telling the truth about what is happening in your life.

Now begin taking action to eliminate items from your list. Where possible, eliminate an item completely. Deal with it to an extent where you can be genuinely happy with how things are and your energy is no longer being drained by frustration and negativity. Depending on your style, you may want to start by eliminating the easiest items on your list, so as to give yourself an experience of success and to build momentum. Alternatively, you may prefer to tackle some of the biggest energy drains first to really free yourself up. Whatever works best for you. Start today to repair the holes in your vase so that you have a more abundant reserve of energy from which to live.

This whole chapter has been about how you can take better care of and sustain yourself, so as to be in good shape for living the adventure of life to the full. You want to have happy, fulfilled companions on your journey, so it makes sense to encourage and support other people also to take care of themselves.

Key points

Part of what gives you personal power is embracing your everyday humanness and giving yourself what it takes really to sustain yourself, whether for the duration of a project or in the long-term for a healthy and fulfilled life.

You can look at this through the mutually-supportive perspectives of:

- Personal Ecology
- Taking Care of Your Needs
- Energy Maintenance

Personal ecology involves seeing yourself as a natural resource to be treated with respect. It means examining your priorities and making choices that preserve your resources rather than squandering them. Relying on adrenalin is not sustainable and leads to stress and burnout.

Taking care of your needs involves understanding the different types of needs and how you are affected when they are, or are not, being met. Only you can say whether, for you, a particular need is essential, desirable or useful.

There are needs associated with each of the different aspects of your being as:

- An organic, physical entity needing nourishment and maintenance
- A feeling, interactive, social person
- A cognitive, thinking person
- An aesthetic, creative and expressive individual
- A spiritual being

You are responsible for getting your needs met, including how you interact with other people. Complaining, as a replacement for actually doing something, keeps you stuck as a victim. Learn to communicate your needs and to make clear requests. In addition, learn to set and maintain appropriate boundaries.

Recognize the symptoms pointing to unmet needs and find new and creative ways of meeting the need in present time. Where necessary, acknowledge and shift any limiting beliefs that are associated with the need.

A lot of what people call thinking consists of mindlessly recycling old ideas and thoughts. Real change requires that you think more consciously and deeply and fully engage with the inquiry. The reflection points throughout the book, are there to help you do this.

Make it about both you *and* other people expressing and getting more of your needs met healthily. Get your needs met from a variety of sources so that you don't put too much pressure on just one person.

For couples, as with other relationships, good communication is essential. Find out what each other's needs are and what helps each of you feel loved. Metaphorically, do your prefer apples or oranges?

In relation to families, it can help to remember the five benefits, to you and others, of getting your needs met:

- You get the direct benefits of self-care and support.
- You give yourself the message that you matter and are valued
- You are in a more resourceful state – others get a better you
- They learn to include another's needs and to work as a team
- You model for them that it is good to appreciate and take care of themselves

The Needs Review is a self test to see how well you are currently getting your different needs met and where you may want to make some changes.

To stay healthy, your energy input must more than balance your energy output. On the one hand, you want to increase your sources of positive energy and, on the other hand, you want to reduce your energy drains. Taking care of your needs is a major part of this.

As well as making rest, exercise and diet important, positive energy habits also include other small things that you do on a daily basis. The list given in the chapter covers the five different aspects of yourself.

Either choose to be genuinely happy with a situation or else do what you can to transform it. Clearing energy drains is one of the fastest and most effective ways of improving your quality of life.

General tips

- Don't try to take care of all of your unmet needs at once
- Use the Needs Review to get started and then continue over time
- Be patient with yourself and keep a sense of humour
- Notice and celebrate all the positive shifts that you make
- Realize and accept that this is not a quick fix. Stay with it
- Encourage other people also to take better care of themselves

Setting intentions

If you need a reminder about holding intentions then take a look at chapter 2.

Possible intentions to hold include:

- Choose to practise personal ecology and to respect your natural resources
- Choose to take responsibility for getting your own needs met
- Choose to increase your score on the Needs Review by 20 points
- Choose to get your physical needs met more fully
- Choose to get your emotional and relatedness needs met more fully
- Choose to communicate more fully in your close relationship
- Choose to get your cognitive and mental needs met more fully
- Choose to get your aesthetic needs met more fully
- Choose to get your creative and expressive needs met more fully
- Choose to get your spiritual needs met more fully
- Choose to increase your sources of positive energy
- Choose to reduce your energy drains

Taking action

Remember, from chapter 2, that actions which come out of raising your awareness and holding an intention to change will be the most powerful. To start with, choose things that are a stretch but not too threatening. Focus on no more than three at any one time. The following actions are some ideas to get you started:

- Cut down on tea and coffee. Choose your limit for the day and stick to it.
- Take the Needs Review and select three needs to focus on
- For each need, set yourself an achievable, one month goal for improvement
- Every day take at least one action for each need
- Go to bed early enough (for you) at least four nights this next week
- Schedule time in your diary, just for taking care of you
- Set and maintain at least two boundaries this next week
- Schedule quality time in your diary to spend with your partner
- Read a good book instead of watching TV
- Spend one hour this week doing something creative
- Spend at least 20 minutes per day connecting with your spiritual source
- Schedule holidays ahead of time
- Keep the weekend free of work-related issues
- Practise at least five positive energy habits each week
- Clear at least two energy drains per week for the next four weeks

4 ~ Empowering Your self

The meaning of empowerment

The term 'empowerment' has been hyped-up and de-valued with jargon over recent years, which is a great shame because the original meaning of the word is practical and … well, empowering!

The two main meanings of 'empowerment' are 'to authorize' and 'to enable'. So empowering yourself involves making yourself the authority on what holds true for you, what you want to do and how you will do it. And it includes giving yourself the support and the means to make it possible.

Claiming your authority

Often our ideas of empowerment are stereotyped, grandiose and infer being like somebody else. If you're a man, you may do the emotional equivalent of pulling your stomach in, looking slightly mean and preparing to do battle. If you're a woman, you may think of donning a power suit and reaching the top.

However, a truly empowered you may choose to have a paunch without apology or to downsize without shame, no matter what other people think. You may want to set and achieve huge goals that bring you acknowledgment and financial success. You may want to make a significant difference to your community. You may want to simplify your life and live quietly without pressure. And you may want to do something else completely different.

As they become more empowered, my clients choose to do less in some areas and to say 'no' to certain people and pressures. They also stretch themselves considerably in other areas that matter to them – not because they *ought* to but because they *want* to and it fulfils them; they value themselves enough to go for it.

So let's distinguish between being empowered and what you choose to do with it, which may, or may not, look like what I or somebody else chooses to do. In other words, we are talking about *your* being empowered to be and to express *you*.

All too often, we give away our authority and allow others to be the 'author' of our life-script. We restrict ourselves and our choices out of fear of what others will think and how they will judge us.

Reflection point   **Letting go of the 'shoulds'**

What would you want to do (or not) if you let go of all 'shoulds' and 'oughts'?

What would a 'less correct' but 'more real' you choose?

Failure as feedback to success

We also let fear of failure prevent us from reaching for the things we want. Many times we don't admit to ourselves, let alone to others, what we do really want. We think that if we did that then we would have to do something about it and we might fail. So it is safer not even to know what we want in the first place. If we had acted this way as babies, we would still be crawling and would never have uttered our first word in case it was wrong!

Failure is not inherently painful or negative. Seen in another light, failure is simply a process of feedback that leads to success. The majority of people who have accomplished a project that matters to them have gone through many setbacks and kept on trying new approaches. They use 'failure' as feedback that a change is needed and not as a sign that they are not okay as a person. Look around and, in general, 'successful' people have experienced far more failures than people we call 'failures'.

When you drop the ball

I used to give classes in the Alexander Technique, for posture and movement, to students on a performance arts course. There is a lot of pressure and competition in the performance world and even though they realized that being relaxed allowed them to perform better it could still be quite a challenge.

To get them used to maintaining a relaxed body awareness, I would teach them some simple three-ball juggling. Initially, they would tense up because their biggest concern was not to drop the ball – to fail, as they saw it. So the first step was to make this not such a big deal. Whenever a student dropped a ball, I got them to turn to the class, relax and say as cheerfully as possible, 'I dropped one!' Of course, being a bunch of performers they played this up beautifully. Then they would casually take their time to pick the ball up and start again. It was a delight to watch uptightness turn to grins as they got used to this perspective. Also to hear how they took this outside the class to auditions and other situations. And, by the way, most of them learned to juggle and to enjoy it.

Next time you find yourself getting uptight or giving yourself a hard time because you got something wrong, try saying with a smile, 'I dropped one!' Then pick yourself up and start again.

Reflection point **Fear of failure**

If you had no fear of failure, what would you attempt that you have been holding back from?

One of the most empowering things is to have a vision or goal that really connects with you and which pulls you forward and motivates you. We'll talk more about that in chapter 7. Here we'll look at what empowers you generally in being and expressing yourself, as you move towards your visions and goals, whatever they may be.

Organizations, families, teams and relationships vary enormously in the extent to which they empower or disempower you in doing your best and enjoying yourself. It makes sense, wherever possible, to choose environments that are empowering. It makes even mores sense to take care of your inner environment and to aim to give yourself what you would ideally want to receive from others.

As stated at the beginning of the chapter, the root meanings of empowerment are firstly to take full authority for your life and secondly to enable yourself to achieve the results that matter to you. In looking at what supports you in this, the following model has been invaluable to me and to many of the people with whom I have worked

The 3 Rs Model of empowerment

- Responsibility – Ownership and Accountability
- Respect – Attitude and Language
- Resources – Time, Things, Skills and People

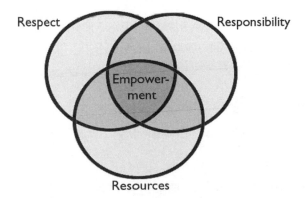

Responsibility

If you work with a professional coach, they will continually encourage you to take responsibility for your choices, your agreements and your experiences. Only by taking responsibility in your life can you claim your authority and realize your potential. Yet there are different perspectives on responsibility that can make it not such an attractive proposition.

Connotations of responsibility

Being given and accepting responsibility has positive connotations – the sense of being respected and considered able, dependable and trustworthy.

There are also the practical connotations of assuming responsibility for a decision, a project or a person. There are agreements and expectations (stated or assumed), accountability and consequences dependent on the outcomes. These are necessary and fine provided that the expectations and assumptions are clear and reasonable (which often they are not) and that the consequences are aimed at positively moving things forward.

Finally, there are the negative connotations of responsibility – such as pointing to who is at fault, who has made a mistake and, worst of all, who is to blame and who should be punished. And whoever that is certainly is NOT okay. This way of thinking is one which I encourage you to let go of.

The aim of this section is to support you in viewing responsibility in a positive context that frees you up to make the most of your life and opportunities.

Three areas of responsibility

Let's explore three areas of responsibility a little further:

- Being responsible for your choices
- Being responsible for a job or a project
- Being responsible for your experiences, including your past

Being responsible for your choices

Individual choices are not made in isolation from the whole of your life, needs, values and priorities. We have seen how important it is to get your needs met so that your choices are less likely to be driven by unmet needs. In the next chapter, on listening to yourself, you will clarify your values which give you a framework for making everyday decisions. Here we look at what is involved in taking responsibility for your choices and how you can do so more consciously and with less angst.

In some limited situations, particularly work-oriented ones, decisions can be made simply on the basis of data and figures or on the basis of pre-agreed criteria established by others. Then, making choices is a question of following procedure. In most situations, however, there is a greater or lesser element of exercising personal judgement and hence having responsibility for the choices made.

The bottom line is that you are always responsible for your choices, whether you want to be or not. If, like the proverbial ostrich, you put your head in the sand and put off making a choice then you have chosen not to choose. If you allow an expert to make choices for you, then you choose which expert to follow and how much to follow them. And if you opt for being a victim then that is still your choice. Of course, some events really are outside your control, but you always have a choice in how you respond to them.

A fundamental characteristic of choice is that every time you choose one option you are saying 'no' to another; this is where the fear comes in. What if another option would have been better? Or, what if somebody else would have chosen better (whatever 'better' might mean)?

Knowing that, whatever you do or don't do, you are still choosing can be liberating if you realize that you can only do the best you can with the understanding and resources available. You are not all-knowing and, in the greater scheme of things, whatever will be will be and tomorrow will be tomorrow. Susan Jeffers, in her book *Feel the Fear and Beyond* (Rider, 2000), emphasizes an outlook of choosing between several good options rather than choosing a sole right one.

Fear of failure and blame can lead you to become paralysed with indecision, which is still a choice. Ho, hum – no getting away from it!

People have different strategies for making decisions. Many of these are influenced more by the desire to avoid responsibility, possible failure and blame than they are by wanting to achieve the best outcome.

Strategies for avoiding blame include:

- Doing what has always been done – responsibility is given over to past practices even though they may be outdated and cause you problems.
- Doing nothing and waiting for things to happen by chance – responsibility is given over to fate, even though choosing not to choose is still a choice.
- Analysing data and information endlessly (analysis paralysis) – responsibility is given over to 'objective fact', even though there is usually some element of risk and the unknown in most decisions.
- Discussing things endlessly with as many people as possible – responsibility is diffused (and everyone gets confused) even though sooner or later one person or group must make a decision.

There is nothing inherently wrong with any of the above approaches. If the way in which you currently do things in a certain area is truly effective, there is no need to fix what isn't broken. Sometimes the wise man or woman knows when to wait and let things unfold. It is important to make informed decisions and get facts as clear as possible, especially when finances are involved (less sure how this works when ordering dinner or choosing a movie …). Getting varied perspectives can throw new light on a problem or an opportunity.

The important distinction to make is whether your motive is primarily one of maximizing the opportunities *or* of avoiding risk and blame associated with possible 'failure'.

The motivation to avoid blame is as common in organizations as it is with individuals. In their book, *The Knowing-Doing Gap* (Harvard Business School Press, 1999), Jeffrey Pfeffer and Robert Sutton explore some of the similar patterns that prevent organizations from learning and taking action.

Reflection point **Making decisions**

How comfortable are you, on a scale of 1-10, with making decisions?

What are your preferred strategies for making decisions?

How do you try to avoid responsibility for your decisions?

Risk is a fact of life and, in some ways, neutral. It simply means that there is some unknown variability of outcome. Successful people tend to be risk-conscious but not risk-averse. They balance the desirability of the possible gains with their ability to manage possible losses. They get all the relevant information and also use their intuition or gut feeling. The risks are acceptable for their resources or situation and, if things don't work out, then they learn from the experience and move on. They do not waste time and energy on blaming themselves. The same is true of some innovative organizations which promote a no-blame culture and empower people to take considered risks.

It is appropriate to be aware of and cautious of risk, provided that you also realize that sometimes avoiding responsibility for decisions is much riskier and can cost you much more. It can also be very energy draining, especially when the decision you end up making is not that important and several options may be satisfactory. It is like going to a restaurant and choosing between the fish, meat or vegetarian options. They may all be good but if you spend all evening only looking at the menu, you will go home hungry. As the saying goes, 'Don't sweat the small stuff – and remember, it's all small stuff.'

Reflection point **Sweating the small stuff**

Where do you sweat the small stuff?

From the menu of life, what meal would you now like to order?

A common scenario, when working with a client, is to find that they have actually already made a decision in their heart. Rather than acknowledge, accept and take responsibility for that decision, they are still trying to 'prove' to themselves that it must work out, and are confusing themselves in the process. If you are in a situation where you know that you have already decided what to do, stop analysing it and driving you and everybody else crazy.

CASE STUDY ~ PHIL

Phil was a marketing executive in the entertainment business. He found that he no longer enjoyed the lifestyle and was out of synch with the culture and values around him. He had been in dispute with a colleague and had the chance to leave with a golden handshake and a good reference. This meant turning his back on his familiar world and the high salary that went with it. It was obvious listening to Phil that, in his heart, he had already decided to leave but he continued to talk about it as if he was really weighing up the options. Apart from the angst this was causing him, it left him in a very un-resourceful space for negotiating his leaving. When he could acknowledge the decision that he had already made, he was able to move ahead and conclude the negotiations gracefully.

Reflection
point   **Knowing what you want already**

Is there is a situation in your life where really you already know what you will do next – and yet continue to go round in circles talking about it?

Talking a decision through with a friend, colleague, coach or mentor can be a very helpful and responsible thing to do, especially when they primarily provide a space for you to think more clearly. Avoid people who habitually try to fix things for you or who undermine your authority to make choices for yourself.

Once you are freer of the fear of failure, and are more ready to accept the unknown element in any decision, there are many approaches to decision making. Listening to yourself, to clarify a situation or to make a decision, is covered in some depth in the next chapter. Here are some simple tools that you can start with.

Some tools for decision making

When choosing between several options:

- Take a page for each option and draw a line down the centre. Write out the pros on one side of the line and the cons on the other. Do any of the choices now stand out?

When choosing between two options:

- Do your research first and then flip a coin. Notice whether you are happy or disappointed with the result. This is simple but can be highly effective.
- Get yourself into a relaxed state and visualize walking along a path which divides into two, one for each choice. Which looks more appealing? Now imagine yourself forward in time and see what each path holds in store. Which now looks more attractive and why? If you enjoy visualizations, visit the members' section at www.self-factor.com.

Being responsible for a job or project

When you are responsible for a job or project there are certain expectations about what you will do and what results you will achieve, as well as about possible consequences if the proposed outcomes are not met. Many problems are the result of expectations and agreements being assumed and not clarified.

You may find that you have somehow been delegated additional responsibility without your agreement or else find yourself saying 'yes' automatically. If you find yourself habitually taking on unreasonable agreements and expectations, you will need to learn to be more assertive, to negotiate agreements that work better for you and to set boundaries on what is acceptable to you. When negotiating agreements keep to what you want and what works for you. Don't try to make the other person admit that they are wrong as this almost never works and is counter-productive.

Boundaries

Here is a reminder of the four step boundary model, introduced in chapter 3:

- Inform the other person of the situation that is not working for you
- Request them to change it
- Let them know the consequences if it continues
- Carry out the consequences

Letting your concerns be known may be sufficient to get changes made but this is not always so and you have the ultimate responsibility for whether or not you put up with things. Unless you are willing to carry out the consequences, don't go into them – otherwise you will only dig yourself into a hole.

Propping up a system that doesn't support you

One common scenario, whether in personal relationships or at work, is what I call 'propping up a system that doesn't support you'. In most work situations, there will be occasional, unforeseen circumstances where everybody willingly puts in the extra hours and pulls through together. This is a positive example of team spirit. If, however, fire-fighting becomes a way of life and the permanent culture is to sacrifice personal time and quality of life to make things work, this is not sustainable and is bad news for everyone. People's loyalty is being abused. This is a symptom of bad management, poor systems or insufficient resources and is most likely a combination of all three. If, after expressing your concerns, things don't change then you may need to make the decision to take care of yourself. Stop propping things up and be willing to allow things to go down the drain until the need for change is seen and accepted by the decision makers. While you keep clearing up the mess, they can keep ignoring the problem. If things still don't change, then take responsibility for your choices, get another job and get a life!

CASE STUDY ~ SARAH

Sarah was an IT lecturer at a small university. Over the previous few years, auxiliary support had been reduced and teaching hours extended without explicit agreement from staff. As a result, Sarah and others found their personal time eroded and stress levels going through the roof. Sarah would routinely collapse with fatigue when the holidays started. When Sarah really understood that she was propping up a system that didn't support her, she started negotiating her new terms' contracts differently. She refused classes that involved excessive amounts of new preparation or which meant her travelling in for only a couple of hours at a time. This meant that the university had to train up other, less-experienced lecturers and give them the extra support. Sarah also reduced the hours she spent marking and did work to a sufficient standard rather than to the level of excellence of which she was capable. She would have preferred the overall level of service to be higher but was no longer willing to sacrifice herself to provide it. For the first time in two years she spent the whole of her Christmas break in good health and enjoying herself.

Even when there is a genuine willingness on all sides, you may falsely assume that everybody has the same understanding and expectations as you. It is worth taking the time to get clear on what the expectations are and to go through the various 'what if' scenarios. This is especially important when going into business with friends or family. There can be a reluctance to question each other and to show the same reasonable caution that you would do with a colleague. The belief seems to be something like this: 'Because we are friends/family we will think the same and agree on how to handle situations when the time comes.' This may be true but many good friendships have suffered from unclear expectations. If you are considering embarking on a business venture with friends or family, I suggest that you brainstorm possible scenarios including the possibility that one of you may want to get out. Find out if you can agree on how you want to deal with things. If you cannot reach a win-win agreement then it's better to settle for no-deal and keep the friendship.

Accountability

Accountability, if thought of as judgement and punishment, is a burden and a further reason to avoid responsibility. However, it can be a supportive process helping you keep your agreements by generating, and responding to, feedback. The more you do what you say you will do, the more confidence you and others have in your word and your ability. In coaching, accountability is used in this way to help clients stay motivated and on track.

Good habits to develop around agreements

When taking or sharing responsibility for a project, good habits to develop are:

- Only agree to things that you are genuinely willing to do
- Clarify agreements and expectations beforehand
- Don't prop up a system that doesn't support you
- Aim for win-win agreements. The next best option is no-deal
- If you, or the other person, break an agreement then sort it out quickly and start again with new, clear agreements
- Use accountability to support you, not as something to beat yourself with

Reflection point **Agreements**

Where and with whom do you need to say 'no' more often?

Where would you benefit from clarifying agreements and expectations?

What situations do you need to change, or else walk away from?

Being responsible for your experiences

Letting go of blame

If you associate responsibility with blame, you will naturally be reluctant to take responsibility for your life and your experiences. You will feel that whatever is wrong is your fault and that this makes you 'not okay'. If you try to get out of this by blaming other people and situations, you may feel a little better about yourself in the short term, but are disempowered from being able to change anything in the long term. (By the way, when I used the word 'disempowered' in my mail program, the spell-checker suggested 'disembowelled' … not so far off!)

The big shift, and the way out of the impasse, is to let go of blame itself and to see both yourself and others as doing the best you all can with the resources and understanding you have at the time.

This is not about condoning poor behaviour in yourself or in them, but rather about separating the behaviour from the basic 'okay-ness' of the person. Part of being empowered is accepting and dealing with the consequences of your actions and you may need to raise your standards as well as to set boundaries and consequences for other people. The point lies in the perspective from which you do this; do you want to make some*body* wrong or do you want to make some*thing* right?

Blame, guilt and regret look backwards and somehow wish that things had never happened. Responsibility starts now, accepts what is and chooses to deal with it as well as possible.

Response-ability

From now on, I invite you to think of taking responsibility in the context of developing response-ability – the ability to respond to what is and to make choices. You can waste a lot of energy wishing that things were different and hoping that somebody or something else would make them different. You don't have to like how things are but only by first accepting the reality of what you are dealing with are you able to respond and to make changes.

It shouldn't be like this …

Frequently, in a coaching conversation, clients will try to gain my agreement that a boss, colleague, client, partner or whoever shouldn't be the way they are. It's as if they feel that, if they can only prove that the other person is 'bad', then some divine force will intervene and put it all to rights. It's like a child complaining to their parents about a sibling and hoping that the parents will take their side. Usually I will give the client a little BMW time to vent their frustrations, to be human and let off steam – BMW standing for 'bitch, moan and whine'. Sometimes I will even ask them how much BMW time they need while reminding them that they are paying for the time! Then I will turn it all back to them by saying something like, 'Okay, you don't like the way they are. I can understand that. Now, given the way they are, how can *you* respond and deal with things?'

You may choose to leave a difficult job or relationship. You may choose to stay and do what you can within your sphere of influence. But what never works is wasting your energy thinking that they or the situation 'should' be different.

Reflection point   **Thinking it 'should' be different**

Where in your life or work are you wasting energy trying to 'prove' that people or things 'should' be different?

How could you make better use of that energy to deal with them the way they are?

Living from the perspective of 'if only it were different' is one of the favourite strategies for victim-hood and unhappiness. How deeply entrenched it can become is illustrated in the following story.

The Elders' Story

The wise elders of a remote tribe gathered together with the aim of increasing the general joy and well-being of the tribe. They decided that the main problem was their tendency to say, 'If only …'. And so they created a ritual to start a new era in their history. The whole tribe took a huge tree trunk and carved the words 'If only' on it. Then they dug a hole twenty feet deep and buried the tree trunk to symbolize that they would never think this way again. A night of celebration and abandon followed, in which many future tribe members were created. All seemed wonderful until one thoughtful elder was heard to say, 'If only we'd buried it more deeply!'

Forgiveness

It can be particularly difficult to accept and respond to 'what is' when you feel that you have been mistreated or that you have mistreated others. Sometimes this needs forgiveness, both of others and of yourself.

Every psychotherapist and spiritual counsellor will tell you about the power of forgiveness, for physical health as well as for peace of mind. 'Easier said than done,' you may say and you would have a point. Please don't pretend to feel okay about something if you don't; phoney smiles on top of gritted teeth don't usually fool anyone and they play hell with your fillings! Reaching acceptance can take time and work. This is particularly true following traumatic experiences, when you may need to go through a process similar to bereavement, and it may help to talk with a trusted friend or with a counsellor. You need to feel whatever you are feeling and not try to coerce yourself into premature acceptance or forgiveness, even though you know logically that, in the end, this is the only solution. Hearts and emotions follow their own logic and process.

Much of the time, however, we are not consciously engaged in this valid healing and growing process but have instead established a habit of blame, guilt and resentment as the backdrop to how we approach life.

Some years ago, I became really conscious of old resentment going through my head about how I had been wronged and what 'they' had done and how 'they' were bad and on and on and on ... . From out of nowhere, I started singing a little song ... 'Duncan is a whinger, a whinger, a whinger. Duncan is a whinger and so say all of us!!' And then I cracked up and had one of the best belly laughs in years.

So next time you find yourself going through your own special litany of wrongs against you, stop and reflect. Are you going through a positive healing process en route to forgiveness and acceptance? Or are you being an habitual whinger? Only you can say, although it can help to get some feedback from a trusted friend. If you suspect that you have been habitually whinging, you can make a big deal about it or else you can laugh at yourself and get on with enjoying life.

And next time you beat your chest in remorse, are you looking to put things right or are you indulging? If you've stolen someone's bicycle then feeling remorse, apologizing and giving it back are in order. If you choose to feel terribly guilty but keep the bicycle, then it's not so convincing …

Tearing up the IOUs

One way or another I am suggesting that you tear up all the old IOUs that you have been carrying. This is the list of people who you feel have done things to you and so now 'owe' you. It is also the list of people that you have wronged and whom you now feel you owe, but don't really want to do anything about. If you do need to do or say something first, or to work with a therapist, then do so. Otherwise just choose to declare all the IOUs null and void.

Reflection point **IOUs**

How long is your IOU list?

What would it take for you to declare it null and void?

My guess is that in our humanness we never stop making up these energy draining IOUs, but we can take them a lot less seriously and tear them up much sooner. It's like clearing a garden. Sometimes we do some clearing or landscaping that makes a big, noticeable change. Sometimes we just need to keep doing the weeding.

Bit by bit you can enjoy taking more and more responsibility for your life and find that this is a liberation rather than a burden. As this gets to be your usual way of looking at life, you will find that playing victim holds much less attraction for you.

Taking responsibility for your choices, agreements and experiences is central to empowering yourself. Alongside this you also need to give yourself respect and to provide appropriate resources.

Respect

In this section you will be encouraged to develop a positive attitude to who you are and to what you can do and have in your life.

Your attitude to yourself

Your attitude to yourself is a reflection and reinforcer of your self image – what you believe about yourself. You may recall from chapter 2 that your beliefs are thoughts attached to corresponding feelings and ways of looking at things. Your belief patterns have been developing since childhood and will have made a certain sense at some point in your life. They are held unconsciously and are reinforced by repetition so as to create the reaction cycle. Our beliefs determine what we put out into the world, the world responds appropriately and we collect evidence that further strengthens our beliefs. For all intents and purposes, it as if there is a part of ourselves that not only continues the old beliefs, whether they serve us or not, but defends them and feels threatened when we step away from them.

We all take on some disempowering beliefs, about life and ourselves, and then forget that we have the ability to re-evaluate and choose the beliefs that we live by. It doesn't have to stay this way.

It is usually unhelpful to fight against beliefs or to attempt to 'prove' that they are wrong and that another belief is now 'the truth'. Overall it works better to see beliefs as assumptions about yourself or about life to which you have given authority. Now you can re-choose which assumptions to energize and align your authority with. This isn't because they are 'the absolute truth' but because you prefer to look at and experience your life from a happier and more helpful perspective.

Changing limiting beliefs

The three aspects of changing belief patterns are:

- Uncovering your present beliefs
- Lessening their power over you
- Trying out new possibilities

One of the most direct ways to find out about your beliefs is to listen to how you talk to and about yourself. Start to notice what you habitually say and how you say it. As someone once said, 'For many of us, if we talked to our friends the way we talk to ourselves then no-one would stick around!'

Reflection
point **Criticism or encouragement?**

What kinds of things do you habitually say to and about yourself?

Do you motivate yourself more by criticism or by encouragement?

Don't be in too much of a hurry to change your self-talk or make a huge fuss about your limiting beliefs. As you become more curious and gently question them you will find that many changes start to happen simply as a result of your compassionate observation. If you get uptight and judge yourself for being negative, the energy of that self-judgement will do you more harm than the original patterns. After all, you have probably had these patterns of thinking for most of your life and you are still here. So you can afford to lighten up and be patient with yourself as you explore and experiment. Bit by bit, you can cultivate beliefs that are more empowering and life-affirming.

Another powerful method of uncovering limiting beliefs is to ask the question (in relation to some issue, person or project), 'What might I be assuming that is limiting me or preventing me from moving forward?' When you identify a limiting assumption that you have bought into, then you can ask yourself, 'What would be a more freeing assumption that I would prefer to live from?' Then explore and play with the different options that occur to you.

CASE STUDY ~ MARJORY

Marjory was a senior marketing consultant who had agreed to an extended six month contract, which meant postponing a new venture which she had been passionate about developing. She was becoming increasingly irritable with staff and found it difficult to concentrate on the work at hand. She uncovered the belief that it was not okay to make mistakes and that you had to suffer for them. For her, a more freeing assumption was that it was okay to make mistakes and to learn from them and that they were not a big deal. From this standpoint she was able to acknowledge that it had been a mistake to accept the contract and that in future she would make decisions based more on her values than on the financial rewards. She was also able to forgive herself and found that she was then able to make the most of and even enjoy the present work.

Reflection point   ***Assumptions***

What is one limiting belief or assumption that you can identify?

What would be a more freeing assumption that you would like to try on?

Choose to 'act as if' this is true and see what you learn.

A third approach to uncovering limiting beliefs is to get together with a friend or friends and look at some of the recurring patterns in your life as if you were looking at somebody else's life. Then ask, 'What might somebody who acts this way tend to believe?' Then think of a role model who would handle these situations well. This can be someone you know, a celebrity or even a fictional character. Now ask, 'What would they tend to believe, how would they approach things and what would they do?' Then experiment with 'acting as if' you were that person.

CASE STUDY ~ NAOMI

Naomi was a coach in training who shared with the group some difficulties she was having at work with team members who consistently undermined her authority and crossed her boundaries. Logically she knew that she was good at her job and each time she backed down on an issue she later realized that she had been right and regretted not standing her ground. Through questioning from the group, she uncovered underlying beliefs that her viewpoint was not worth listening to and that others knew better. She had always admired Eleanor Roosevelt for her self-belief and composure and agreed to 'be Eleanor Roosevelt' for the week. She reported back the following week that not only did she feel more confident and act differently but that others picked up on it and didn't challenge her so much in the first place.

Reflection point   *Using a role model*

Think of a current challenge in your life and then think of a role model who would handle the situation well.

How would they approach things and what would they do?

Experiment with 'being them' in the situation.

Summary of ways to change beliefs

Here is a summary of the above and other complementary, mix and match, strategies that you can experiment with. They all lessen the power and compulsion of limiting beliefs and free you up to explore different ways of thinking and behaving.

- Just notice and observe the thoughts and beliefs in your self-talk and the way that they limit your options. Be curious and listen to the tone of voice and tempo as if you were appreciating a good actor in a melodrama (which is quite close to what is happening). Don't try and force yourself to change anything: just notice. You may even find yourself laughing or enjoying the quality of the performance!

- Become genuinely curious. Dialogue with yourself and gently question the assumptions. Some helpful questions include:
  - 'Is this really true?'
  - 'How does it serve me to think this way?'
  - 'What are the implications of thinking this way?'

- In relation to a particular situation or challenge, ask yourself, 'What might I be assuming that is preventing me from achieving my outcome or moving forward with this?'

- Emphasizing that beliefs are a choice rather than a given truth, explore other assumptions (beliefs) that might be more helpful. You can ask yourself:
  - 'What would be a more freeing assumption for me at this time?'
  - 'What would I really like or even love to believe?'
    - → With both these questions, don't get too logical. Go with your first, intuitive response. Look for a wording that resonates with you and gives you a feeling of expansion and wanting to move forward.

- Building on this last approach, you can then explore the new options that arise from trying on a new assumption/belief.

- Once you have identified a more helpful or preferred assumption, ask yourself:
  - 'If I knew that this were true, what would I do next?

- Use the analogy of being the actor in your own play and decide that, for a given period of time, you are going to 'act' the part of a role-model who has more freeing beliefs. Try it out and see what you learn.

- Repeat affirmations of the new belief or write them out on cards and pin them up where you will see them often. If you use affirmations, remember that you are not trying to convince yourself of the truth. Rather you are reminding yourself to explore life from a different and more helpful perspective.

Positive self-talk

Coming back to your self-talk, choose to treat yourself with respect, not only in what you say to yourself but in how you say it. Remember that this not something that you 'should' do. It is something that you want to do because you care about your quality of life. An interesting experiment for a week is to choose not to criticize yourself. You can still decide that you want to do something differently or better, but give yourself feedback positively and constructively instead of with the put-down of criticism. Remember that, even when your behaviour is off or can be improved on, you as a person are fine and deserve to be treated with respect by everyone, starting with yourself. If you realize that you are back in critical mode, don't criticize yourself for being critical! Congratulate yourself for noticing and start again.

CASE STUDY ~ GEORGE

George was head of the IT department in a large community college. He ran the department very efficiently and had lots of new ideas for the college intranet. However, he found that other members of staff were unreceptive and responded with technophobia. As we worked together, it became apparent that George was extremely self-critical and compensated for his supposed shortcomings by relying on technical detail to prove that he was okay. I gave him the exercise of stopping motivating himself with criticism and using encouragement instead. At first he found this quite a challenge but he persevered. Gradually he became much gentler, more self-supportive and stopped trying so hard to prove himself. He found that he developed better and warmer relationships and that others felt freer to express their own doubts and fears around technology. He was then able to reassure them and to come up with simpler systems to support them.

Language patterns

There are also some common language patterns that we use to limit ourselves (see examples on opposite page). There will be times when they are fine and appropriate but most of the time we use them to avoid responsibility and choice. Don't be dogmatic about them or start correcting other people. Just start to notice them and the effect that they have on you and then experiment with replacing them with one of the suggested alternatives.

The old patterns encourage you to think of yourself as powerless, at the mercy of the outside world and with no choice. The alternatives emphasize possibility and taking responsibility for your choices.

For instance, if you say that you will 'try' to go to the gym next week, what does this really mean? If you care enough, you will be there. If you don't care that much then just admit it and say so. Saying you will 'try'

Language Pattern	Alternatives
I'll try to …	I will / I might / I choose to / I choose not to …
I should / I ought to / I have to …	I could / I want to / I choose to / I choose not to …
I've got to …	I could / I get to …
Why is this happening?	What is happening? / how is this happening? What can I do? / how can I do it?
It's not fair / It shouldn't be this way	How will I deal with this?
… but …	… and …

to go leaves you sitting on the fence without taking any responsibility for the choice. There are situations where you give it your best shot and the outcome is outside your control but most times that we use the word 'try' it is an evasion of responsibility for things that are within our control.

The patterns are all examples of how words and phrases carry energy that affects how resourceful and empowered you feel. Don't get uptight about them or start worrying that every negative thought is going to carry a death wish. Some times you will need to be human, to complain and vent your feelings before getting on with leading the good life. Bit by bit though, clean up your thinking and create an overall positive emphasis as a backdrop to your life.

Respect for yourself means having a positive attitude to who you are and what you can do and have in your life. When you are working towards a particular goal it is really important that you respect yourself and have a positive attitude of 'I can and will achieve this'. Other aspects of achieving a goal or vision are considered in the ANSWERS model in chapter 7.

Positive thinking alone is limited in the long term. The thoughts need to be supported by changes in the other areas of the creation cycle. They need to be energized with feelings of expectancy, grounded in appropriate action, supported by positive environments and reinforced by the experiences that you choose to notice and emphasize.

Applying it to organizations

This is as true for organizations as it is for individuals. They may, for instance, decide to change their thinking and create a corporate identity that emphasizes innovation, customer service and long term relationships. But this will have little real effect if behaviours and structures are not changed to align with it. Many companies still rely on fear and internal competition to motivate their sales staff, and this is backed up with monthly bonuses or prizes for the best individual results. There are a number of possible downsides to this approach: when there is one 'winner' you have a whole lot of 'losers', which undermines general morale; successful strategies are jealously guarded rather than shared with others; there tends to be low company loyalty and a market trend to head-hunt rather than develop staff internally. The flip side is that you are equally likely to lose your best sales person to a higher bidder. The overall result, whatever the mission statement may now say, is that short term sales are still emphasized over customer service and long term relationships. To make real change happen, the systems and behaviours will need to emphasize and reward cooperation, teamwork and a focus on long term results.

We've considered Responsibility and Respect. Now we look at the third R in the 3 R model: Resources.

Resources

In a work environment, for somebody to be empowered to do a certain job not only do they need responsibility and respect, but they also need the necessary time, equipment, skills and support. The same is true of you, in whatever you undertake. All too often, though, we set ourselves up for failure by not taking care of the resources we need, or in setting ourselves unrealistic time scales. It is like trying to run a marathon with no preparation and wearing work boots. And the same is true of improving communication, starting a business, writing a book or any other thing that you care about achieving. Without the appropriate resources, you may be setting yourself up for failure.

Personal resources

We have considered a wide range of personal resources under getting your needs met in chapter 3. In the context of this chapter, it is important to realize that getting your needs met doesn't just help you feel better. It is the basis for being effective in whatever you undertake and for how you contribute to any team effort. To use a musical analogy, *you* are the primary instrument through which you play your particular music and hence play your part in the orchestra. Without you there is no music.

Time management

One of the things that people most often cause themselves problems with is how they manage time or, to be more accurate, how they manage themselves in relation to time. Time carries on regardless and is not the problem. How you are and what you do as the seconds, minutes, hours and days roll by is where the challenge and the opportunity lies. Time management is an important area to consider and I highly recommend reading a good book and/or going on a course. (Some are mentioned in the resources section at www.self-factor.com.) Here we will look briefly at some of the areas that crop up frequently in coaching conversations and give you a few tools to explore.

Choosing what to spend time on

When we looked at making decisions, earlier in the chapter, we saw that every choice, however positive, involves letting go of something else. This can lead to the fear of making a bad choice and hence missing out. Rather than taking responsibility for consciously choosing, many people use a variety of strategies to try and postpone, or otherwise evade, the realities of how much time they have available and how much they can actually do with it. There is a myth that if you can only become effective enough then you should be able to do everything you want, regardless. How you use your time is analogous to how you spend your money; you can become a very good and efficient shopper, knowing the best places to shop and the best bargains available. However, if you don't want to get overdrawn, and eventually go bankrupt, you must still take on board how much money you have to spend and how much things cost. Where the analogy breaks down is that you have the possibility of earning or inheriting more money and hence of having more money to spend. Your time available in any one period is fixed.

Let's say that, depending on your particular rhythm, you are alert enough to do things effectively between 7.45 in the morning and 10.00 at night, seven days per week. That gives you near enough 100 hours to 'spend' on everything you do. If your work hours are Monday to Friday, nine until six, then this amounts to 45 hours per week and leaves you 55 hours for everything else, including travel and all the background chores such as shopping, cooking and cleaning. When you spend more time on one thing, such as bringing work home in the evenings or on the weekend, then you have less time to spend on other things, such as yourself or your family. And if you waste a lot of time on things that you don't really care about, you have less time available for the things that you do care about. It's very simple when you start to think about it. Just as with money, if you want to make the best use of your time, you need to budget it well.

CASE STUDY ~ ANNA

Anna was a single mother, with two children, who worked full-time as an accountant for a large charity. She was also taking a distance learning course, developing a new career in consultancy and was in the process of acquiring her second property to renovate and then rent out as part of a long term plan to develop a property portfolio. I asked her if she might also like to buy a little cape, wear her underpants outside her tights and fly over the city putting fear into the criminal fraternity …. She laughed and realized how much she was trying to play out the 'Superwoman' role which many professional women have bought into. Unfortunately, it often takes illness or other disasters for them to stop and take stock. Not surprisingly, Anna felt tired and overwhelmed much of the time and procrastinated on many of her projects. Her usual strategy was to call herself lazy and attempt to do even more. Like many people, Anna had a completely unrealistic perspective on how much time she had available and how long things actually took. She started to let go of some of her unrealistic assumptions and to embrace her humanness more. Alongside this, she learned to be more realistic about her time resources, learned to say 'no' to things and to accept that every new project she took on meant letting go of something else.

As with Anna, it may be enough for you simply to reflect on the realities of time for you to start to make more grounded choices in how you spend it. Tell the truth about what is or is not working for you. If you find yourself continuing to put your head in the sand, and postponing making choices, it will be helpful for you to create a detailed time budget for the week. If you enjoying analysing and planning then you may like to do this anyway.

Creating a time budget

Here is an exercise that I sometimes give to clients to help them appreciate how much time they have available and how they choose to spend it:

Make a list of all the different roles and areas that you take on in your life, such as manager, educator, householder, parent, lover, friend, social person, etc. Under each role, list the different things that you would want to do in a week. For each item, note whether it is primarily work-related or personal, and estimate how much time it will take to do it well. Then total the work and non-work hours and see what your expectations amount to. Below is a layout you can use for this. (It is taken from a spreadsheet that you can find at the members' section at www.self-factor.com. You can download it from the web site, copy it from the book or make your own version.) If the categories used here don't fit for you, amend them. Enter your estimates under the first three columns. The last three columns you can use later, after keeping a time log.

The first time clients fill this in, it is not uncommon for the things they expect to accomplish in a week to require 170 hours or more. If your total comes to more than 100 hours, it is time to start making choices and to let go of some of the things on your list. Keep adjusting what you put down until your choices come within the available budget of 100 hours.

Having created your budget to fit within the available 100 hours, the next step is to see how realistic it is by comparing it to the time that you actually spend on things.

Knowing how much time things take

In order to manage your money well, alongside knowing how much you have to spend you also need to know how much different items cost, including any extra charges such as delivery, tax and insurance. In the same way, when you are budgeting your time, you need to have a realistic idea

Layout for doing your time budget

Role/Area	Activity	ESTIMATED HOURS			ACTUAL HOURS		
		Mon/Fri 9-6	Other	Total	Mon/Fri 9-6	Other	Total
Work Role 1	1						
	2						
	3						
Work Role 2	1						
	2						
	3						
Breaks	lunch						
	tea						
	dinner						
Travel	various						
Personal	reading						
Development	other						
Domestic	cleaning						
	shopping						
	cooking						
	maintenance						
	garden						
Partner	one to one						
Family	1						
	2						
	3						
Social	various						
Creativity	various						
Health	showering						
	exercise						

		ESTIMATED HOURS			ACTUAL HOURS		
Role/Area	Activity	Mon/Fri 9-6	Other	Total	Mon/Fri 9-6	Other	Total
health, continued	other						
Leisure	hobby 1						
	hobby 2						
	reading						
	TV						
	spacing out						
Other	1						
	2						
	3						
TOTAL							
POSSIBLE		45	55	100			

of how long things really take, including any associated activities such as research, planning, communicating with other people and the myriad little extras that usually crop up. Even a relatively uncomplicated hour's workout at the gym may take closer to two hours of your time when you add on packing your bag, travel each way, and a shower afterwards.

The majority of people are wildly optimistic and unrealistic when it comes to estimating how long things take. They also underestimate just how much time gets used up with unimportant trivia such as non-relevant emails. A very helpful exercise is to keep a daily time log for a week. A sample template is shown on page 110 with the time broken down into 20-minute segments. (This is available to download from the members' area at www.self-factor.com. Alternatively, you can copy it or make something similar for yourself.)

For each 20-minute period, briefly describe the activity and put a tick in the relevant category box alongside it. The three categories shown stand for:

- **W**ork time that was necessary, worthwhile or enjoyable
- **P**ersonal time that was necessary, worthwhile or enjoyable
- **L**ost time that was *not* necessary, worthwhile or enjoyable

Don't get judgemental or unrealistic here and start categorizing every activity without a clear purpose as lost time. We all need some downtime for relaxation, integration and relationship building. So a tea break or social chat at work may be both enjoyable and worthwhile in the bigger picture. At home, some good mind-blobbing time with a favourite TV soap may be both relaxing and enjoyable. The time that is neither necessary nor worthwhile *and* which you don't enjoy is lost time.

You can get lots of useful information from keeping a time log this way. How much detail you go into is up to you. By totalling the different category columns, you can see immediately how much of the time you spend is primarily work, personal or lost. To get even more from the time log, you can compare what you have actually done with your previous estimates on the time budget and then fill in the last three columns of the budget.

When clients go through this whole process it can be quite a reality shock to start with. They begin to realize that one of the most effective time management techniques is learning to say 'no', both to other people and to their own ill-considered uses of time. Afterwards, they are in a much better position to make choices and to create realistic schedules.

Once you have a better grip on what you can and want to spend time on, you can look at how to schedule your time and how to use it effectively.

Scheduling time

There is no one system that suits everyone, so if you already have an approach that works for you, stick with it. The most common time

Name:		Day:			Date:					
Time	Activity	Categories			Time	Activity		Categories		
		W	P	L				W	P	L
7.00					3.00					
8.00					4.00					
9.00					5.00					
10.00					6.00					
11.00					7.00					
12.00					8.00					
1.00					9.00					
2.00					10.00					

period to schedule, in any depth, is weekly. At a minimum, an effective system needs to take into account:

- Priorities and deadlines
- Unexpected occurrences
- Appointments with other people
- Time scheduled for specific tasks
- Time for free-flowing, necessary tasks

Here are a few general tips to get you started. Adjust them to suit your style.

- Bearing in mind what we have already looked at, you will need to make choices as to what really is important to you and what you can realistically do. Where other people are involved, you will need to negotiate workable agreements.

- Some things will need to be prioritized to be done first, either because of agreements with other people or because you have a deadline to meet. If you have a deadline for a project, you may want to manage it by chunking it down into smaller tasks and setting deadlines for each of these.

- Appointments with other people, and tasks with a deadline, can be allocated specific time in your diary. Also allocate specific times for connecting with yourself, visioning, planning, and the other necessary quality items that, while essential for effectiveness, often get lost as other things take over.

- Identify times of the day which are better suited to one activity than another. For instance, you might find that immediately after lunch, when many people have a bit of a slump and meetings are less effective, is a good time for you to get on with free-floating activities and to use power bursts to keep you going.

- Don't schedule back to back. Instead, leave plenty of time slots for unforeseen occurrences and free-flowing items. Free-flowing items are things like admin which, while they can be left for a while, are nevertheless essential. Left for too long and you have an overflowing email box, unanswered phone messages and papers all over the place.

- Continually re-assess and update your system and your schedules. Systems are great provided that they fit and support what you actually do. What often happens is that a system is found, in practice, to not quite work. So you do things another way. However, the practical realities learned are not taken into account and the old system is still used for planning and training purposes. This is a particular problem in organizations where a task becomes person-dependent and nobody else knows how to do it. If the person leaves or is away then the replacement struggles with a system that doesn't work. The solution is to make updating the system a part of the job.

Effective use of time

Here again there are different strokes for different folks and it is helpful to try a number of approaches and find out what works for you. Here are a few suggestions, some of which are complementary and some of which you will have to choose between.

- Start any time period by previewing, planning and writing down what you intend to do, using only as much detail as is helpful.

  o At the beginning of the week, list your different areas of concern, review what is already scheduled, plan what you realistically intend to accomplish and complete the week's schedule.

  o At the start of each day, review your schedule and adjust it as necessary.

  o For each individual time slot, jot down a few keywords or bullet points for what you intend doing in this time. For instance, suppose I have a two-hour slot, to deal with free-flowing activities. I might choose three things to focus on, such as clearing my email inbox, dealing with phone calls and getting accounts up to date.

- Deal with the items you don't feel like doing first, rather than putting them at the end of the queue. By dealing with them first, you eliminate the sense of impending doom and get a feeling of accomplishment. Then the things that you prefer doing come as a kind of reward and are an incentive to get the unpleasant items over with. In reverse, if you start with the things that you like doing, you will be motivated to take as long as possible over them so as to postpone the other, less pleasant tasks.

- Chunk big tasks and projects down into smaller, more manageable, mini-projects. This is less daunting and gives you a series of small completions and successes to celebrate, rather than feeling lost in something that seems never ending. For each mini-task, create a checklist of items to complete. Then, even if you only have a short period of time available, you can still complete and tick off one item on the checklist.

- Rather than working from a general 'to do' list, allocate anything you want to do to one of these checklists. Generalized 'to do' lists are limitless and give you the feeling of being on a never-ending treadmill. Working with checklists allows you to feel that you are moving forward with a particular project.

- Where possible, complete one item on a checklist before moving on to something else. Then you can file work away and keep a clear space.

- In contrast to this last suggestion, there is a technique where you work in short, timed power bursts of, say, 20 minutes. Let's use the previous example, of having a two-hour time slot to do admin and choosing to focus on clearing your email inbox, dealing with phone calls and getting your accounts up to date. You list the three items and, starting with the emails, do as much as you can in 20 minutes. At the end of 20 minutes you stop wherever you are and move onto the phone calls. At the end of the next 20 minutes you finish the phone calls (though not by hanging up on someone …) and move onto your accounts. And so you continue cycling between the three activities every 20 minutes. Not only does this help with overcoming procrastination (you only have to do 20 minutes on something), it also helps concentration and uses the mini-deadline to help you get more done. I often find that, working with this system, I get more done in one twenty-minute burst than I might have done in an hour without a committed end point. For this factor to kick in, you must be disciplined in stopping as soon as possible when the twenty minutes is up. Towards the end of your two-hour period, allow some time for clearing up and putting things away, if necessary.

Other people and your time

If you are now ready to make choices, have a realistic view of how long things take and are able to work more effectively, then you are well under way to making good use of the time available to you. However, your good intentions are still likely to get lost unless you can also deal effectively with other people and their demands. Here are a few tips for dealing with other people:

- We looked earlier in the chapter at taking responsibility for the agreements that you do or do not make with other people. Being able to say 'no' and to set healthy boundaries are two of the most effective time management techniques. Without them, you are at the mercy of how other people choose to use up your time for you.

- If you are a manager, there is a healthy balance to be kept between an 'open door' and a 'closed door' policy. This can be literal, if you have your own office or space, or it can simply refer to the times when you are, or are not, available for others to interact with. A certain amount of 'open door' time makes you approachable, helps relationships and keeps you up to date with what is going on. Too much of it and you can be constantly interrupted and have no quality time to focus on your own things. What has worked for many clients is to designate specific times when they are unavailable, unless there is an emergency, and to educate the people around them to respect that. People can leave a note or come back later at one of the times that you are available. This can also be helpful in relationships and families. You claim particular times for yourself, when you are not to be interrupted unless there is an emergency.

• Use the SAID model to reduce unnecessary interruptions and to stop you from taking on problems that don't belong to you.

What's being SAID?

A common scenario is that of taking on somebody else's problem without even realizing that it has happened. Metaphorically, it is as if somebody walks up to you with a monkey on their back and engages you in conversation. At the end of the interaction you find that you have now got the monkey and they walk away unburdened. A tool I have developed for handling this is the SAID model. When someone wants to talk with you, clarify whether what they want from you is:

- S upport – that it is appropriate to come to you for
- A dvice – that it is appropriate to come to you for
- I nformation – that it is appropriate to come to you for
- D ecision – that it is appropriate to come to you for

Anything else is likely to be an attempt to delegate their responsibility and hand you a monkey.

CASE STUDY ~ DANIEL

Daniel had recently been promoted to head of department, at the head office of a nationwide retail business. He knew that he was now expected to take on a leadership role and develop his team. However, he was used to being a hands-on manager and found it difficult not to take over the problems which his direct reports constantly brought to him. With coaching, he introduced the SAID model to his team. Before they came to him with an issue, they had to be ready to say what they wanted from the conversation and to have asked themselves whether he was the appropriate person to come to. At the start of any interaction, he asked them again what they specifically wanted from it. Over a month or so, as everyone got used to this approach, Daniel found that interruptions were far less frequent and took less time. And his team were developing more self-reliance and confidence.

Underlying beliefs about time and structures

When you are familiar with good time management practices, and yet still find it difficult to apply them, it may be that you have some underlying belief patterns that are sabotaging you. Any major change of habit means stepping outside your comfort zone and, as we saw in chapter 2, this may bring up resistance. It is helpful to remember that the part of you which is resisting usually has some kind of positive intention, even if this no longer suits you or if the strategy is outdated and ineffective.

CASE STUDY ~ GLORIA

Gloria was a senior executive in local government who, despite having been on more than one time management course, procrastinated on projects, indulged in time-wasting diversions and had poor boundaries with other people. She resisted putting structures in place and, as a result, worked late most evenings and took work home over the weekend. She couldn't understand why she was sabotaging herself. We explored this together and she realized that her unconscious belief was that, by resisting or sabotaging structures, she would gain more freedom and hence happiness. When we looked at how true this really was, and at the consequences of holding this belief, it became apparent that this approach was actually taking away her freedom and making her very stressed and unhappy. With this understanding, her attitude changed and she now finds it easier to work with structures and to manage her use of time.

This idea of having immediate or short term freedom *from* something is very common and limiting. It is much more empowering to see the bigger picture and to focus on having freedom *for* things that really matter to you.

Reflection point   **Using your time well**

How well do you use your time?

What habits do you need to let go of?

What habits would you like to develop?

What assumptions might be holding you back from using your time well?

What assumptions would be more freeing?

Alongside managing the resource of time, you also need the appropriate equipment, skills and people to support you with any project that you are engaged in.

The things you need

Trying to do a job without the necessary equipment is time-wasting, ineffective and frustrating. Some times you have to make do with what you've got but, where possible, value yourself enough to get or to ask for what you need.

Developing your skills

Additionally, if you really want to do something, be prepared to invest time and energy in developing the skills necessary for you to have a good chance of success. These can be technical skills, 'soft' people skills, or qualities like patience and persistence. This is not about becoming a better person. It is about caring enough about yourself to give yourself the best chance.

This is particularly important if you are looking to develop your career or to start your own business. Here is a strategy for preparing for a new role:

- Do an inventory of all your transferable skills (A)
- Contact someone who already does what you want to do
- Interview them and find out what skills the new role requires (B)
- Compare (A) and (B) and identify the new skills you will need
- Develop the new skills yourself or find someone else to supply these skills

If you are wanting to advance within your present company, and have a supportive H.R. department, then be pro-active and get their help with career planning and training. If you are looking to move elsewhere, think ahead. Consider what skills you will need to have under your belt beforehand and what skills you could reasonably expect to be trained in by a new organization.

And, if you want to start your own business, it is very important that you start planning in this way. A lot of people start a business because they have a product or a service that they love to deliver and they want the freedom and profits that they hope will come from working for themselves. Many such businesses fail because the owners focus on the things they already know how to do and enjoy, while essential auxiliary roles of management, admin, sales and marketing are not taken care of properly. If you want to run your own business successfully, either develop these skills yourself or make sure that you have someone on your team who can do them for you.

The people you need

Alongside having people to support you with their knowledge and skills, you also need them to support you personally. The people, environments and structures around you need to align with your positive beliefs and self-image. It's going to be hard work choosing to see yourself as a wonderful and capable person if you hang out with people who think you're a loser! And if they see themselves as losers then they are not going to be so happy for you when you are doing well. So start to treat yourself in line with your desired self-image and spend time with people and in environments that really support you.

Key points

Empowering yourself means taking authority for your life and enabling yourself to do what you want. We often limit ourselves by giving away our authority and by being afraid of failure.

The 3 Rs model of Empowerment

- Responsibility – Ownership and Accountability
- Respect – Attitude and Language
- Resources – Time, Things, Skills and People

Used positively, responsibility is about developing response-ability. The ability to respond to what is and to do the best you can with it.

Learn to take responsibility for:

- Your choices
- Your agreements
- Your experiences

Make choices for the best outcome rather than to avoid blame. Be risk conscious, rather than risk averse, and don't sweat the small stuff.

Only agree to things that you are genuinely willing to do and clarify agreements and expectations beforehand. Aim for win-win agreements with 'no-deal' as the next best option. If you or they break an agreement, clear it up quickly and start again. Don't prop up a system that doesn't support you.

Accept responsibility for your experiences, past and present. Focus on making things right rather than making people wrong. If you need to do or say something to be clear with the past, then do it or get some help with doing it. Otherwise choose to tear up all the old IOUs and focus on improving the present and the future.

Be respectful to yourself and about your potential. Develop positive attitudes based on life-affirming beliefs about yourself and what is possible.

Changing limiting beliefs involves:

- Uncovering your present beliefs
- Lessening their power over you
- Trying out new possibilities

There are a number of complementary approaches for doing this included in the chapter.

Positive thinking alone is not enough. It needs to be energized with feelings of expectancy, grounded in appropriate action, supported by positive environments and reinforced by the experiences that you choose to notice and emphasize. In addition, avoid limiting language patterns, such as 'I'll try to ... ' and 'I should ...' and replace them with positive alternatives.

Provide yourself with the necessary resources, including time, equipment, skills and support. Give yourself the best chance of success by providing yourself with the right equipment. Also get the best support you can from other people.

Realize that you have a limited amount of time available and that you will need to make choices in how you spend it. Being able to say 'no' to other people, and to some of your options, is the most important time management technique. Alongside this, learn to estimate accurately how long things will really take.

Your weekly schedule needs to allow for priorities and deadlines, unexpected occurrences, appointments with other people, specific projects and free-floating tasks.

There are various tips given for scheduling, using time effectively and dealing with other people. You may also need to shift some beliefs around how you use your time.

Develop the skills you need, particularly when looking to change roles or to start a business. Compare the skills you will need with those that you already have. Then either acquire the missing skills yourself or get the support of someone who has them.

General tips

- Be patient with yourself and know that you are okay to start with
- Have a sense of humour and realize that you don't have to be perfect
- Become curious about what you are currently doing, including your assumptions and how you talk to yourself

- Play with different options. Change your self-talk etc., but don't be rigid
- Notice and celebrate all the positive shifts that you make

Setting intentions

If you need a reminder about holding intentions then take a look at chapter 2.

- Possible intentions to hold include:
- Choose to empower yourself generally in your life and in relation to any particular project you are currently involved with.
- Choose to be the authority in your own life and to make choices according to your own values – not because of what other people will think.
- Choose not to be limited by the fear of failure; choose to see failure as a process leading to success.
- Choose to take responsibility and to develop response-ability in different areas of your life.
- Choose to have clear agreements with people.
- Choose to release the past and to focus on the present and future.
- Choose to be respectful in how you speak to yourself and to be respectful of your potential.
- Choose to provide yourself with the resources you need to support you, both generally and for a specific project.
- Choose to make good use of the time available to you.

Taking action

Remember, from chapter 2, that actions which come out of raising your awareness and holding an intention to change will be the most powerful.

To start with, choose things that are a stretch but not too threatening. Focus on no more than three at any one time.

The following actions are some ideas to get you started:

- Start one activity that you have held back from because you were afraid of what other people might think or say.
- Take on a project that you have held back from because you were afraid of failing.
- Every day for a week, take at least one risk that stretches your comfort zone.
- Do the exercise from the chapter on tearing up the IOUs. Preferably get a friend to do it with you.
- For one week, don't say 'yes' to anything that you don't want to do. Make sure that you follow through on anything you do say 'yes' to.
- In relation to a goal or project, ask yourself what you might be assuming that is hindering your progress – and what might be a more freeing assumption you would like to live from. Then, for one week, 'act as if' that were true.
- As an experiment, for the next week, let go of criticizing yourself and only use positive encouragement. If you find yourself being critical, don't make a big deal about it. Applaud yourself for noticing and just start again.
- Each week for the next 2 months, change at least one thing in your environment to make it more supportive. This could include things such as replacing a faulty piece of equipment, decorating, or not spending so much time with somebody who drains your energy.
- Fill in your time budget and keep a time log over a week.
- Develop and use your own system for scheduling your week
- Practise using the SAID model to eliminate unnecessary interruptions.
- Plan ahead and develop your skills on an ongoing basis. Select one new skill to develop over the next month.

5 ~ Listening to Your Self

The intention of this chapter is to encourage you really to listen to and appreciate yourself – to recognize the vast amount of experience, strength and wisdom that is yours to tap into, if you take the time and make it important enough. Because you are multi-faceted, there are lots of different sides of yourself to connect with and lots of different approaches for doing so. I will offer a selection of methods for you to try out and hopefully you will become excited at the possibilities and continue to explore other books and resources.

Don't get bogged down in the specific techniques, however helpful; they are just tools for accessing your own answers and solutions. The bottom line is to keep asking yourself the core questions that, one way or another, this book has been prompting you to address:

- What is really true for you?
- What do you really want?
- What is the best way forward for you?

Listening to yourself is central to having a good relationship with yourself, and hence making the most of your life and opportunities. It interlinks with and supports the other aspects of the SELF model – Sustaining, Empowering and Friendship.

You cannot sustain yourself if you don't know what you need. All too often we censure awareness of our needs in accordance with what is acceptable to others and to our own, socialized self-image. In so doing, we deny and suppress many aspects of ourselves that, if taken care of, would support us more in everything we do.

You cannot empower and respect yourself if you don't know who and what is there to be empowered and respected. You cannot use your strengths if you don't know them and you cannot gain the satisfaction and impetus of living aligned to your values and vision if you don't know what they are. If you don't listen to yourself, you risk living from scripts and 'shoulds' which may sound good but leave you feeling hollow and dissatisfied.

And you cannot offer yourself friendship if you are not ready to listen. That is part of what friends do.

While, strictly speaking, listening implies hearing sounds or words, I use the term more broadly to include anything where you pay close attention to, connect with and give importance to what is going on with you and what you are about. You can listen to your words or thoughts and you can also listen to your feelings, intuitions, and anything else that results in your knowing yourself more fully. When you notice something, you may then articulate it in words by asking yourself, 'What is this telling me?'

Listening can involve putting special time aside to tune-in and connect with yourself. It can also take place in the activity of everyday life, when you pay attention to your responses to situations and to what you really think, feel, need and want. Deep listening is not passive: it requires intention and commitment.

Aspects of good listening

The experience of being listened to

Let's start by considering what it is like really to be listened to by another person.

Reflection point   **Experience of listening**

Remember a time when you really felt listened to.

What was the experience like? What did you feel?

What supports really effective listening?

What gets in the way of deep listening?

I often ask these questions of coaches in training. Here are some typical responses.

Experiences of being really listened to include:

Safety, space, acceptance, being understood, love, connection, being okay, being fully heard and seen as unique, being validated, hearing yourself more clearly, finding out about yourself, being cared about, a sense of relaxation and peace, being empowered.

The things that contribute really to listening to someone include:

Valuing the person, patience, being fully present, genuine interest, lack of judgement, making enough time, lack of agenda on the part of the listener, ability to hear and reflect back what is said, confidentiality, caring about them.

Obstacles to real listening include:

Outside distractions, time pressure, an agenda of what should be being said or present, rehearsing a reply rather than just being present and listening, wanting to fix the person, thinking about something else, presuming you already know what is going to be said.

It becomes evident that the experience of really being listened to is a wonderful and yet rare gift in today's busy world. And so it makes it particularly important that you learn to listen to yourself, as well as learning to listen to others.

Listening for coaches

As you go through this book, you are learning to coach yourself and the heart of good coaching is listening. Here is a top ten of listening tips I give to coaches.

Top 10 tips for becoming a better listener

Attitude

1. Develop a deep respect for people and their uniqueness. Realize that, however much experience you have had, you have never listened to THIS person at THIS time before. Become deeply fascinated by people.

2. Develop a deep respect for people's ability to find and commit to their own solutions. Being really heard can, in itself, be a very powerful and empowering experience.

3. Develop a deep respect for the power of synergy and for your intuitions that come about as a result of connecting through listening. This may seem paradoxical to the previous point. You do have perspectives to offer people. The key point is whether you NEED to do that or can offer it as appropriate.

Ways of Listening

4. Listen TO what is being said well enough that you could reflect it back using the same language and phrases. We all need to feel that our story is heard and acknowledged the way we present it.

5. Listen WITH them. Be able to step into their shoes and connect with them as fellow human beings beyond the words and the situation.

6. Listen FOR all the different information that is being presented in words, nuances, tones of voice and silences. This includes the current and desired reality, strengths and values, motivations (positive and negative), recurring patterns, unmet needs and more.

Skills to Develop

7. Practise listening to, and taking care of, yourself so that your own needs are met and you are able to be fully present as you listen to another. This includes being free of the need to 'fix' people. Then you can focus on THEIR agenda rather than your own.

8. Become comfortable with silence AND, at the same time, don't rely on it. A pause at the end of what has been said can often encourage someone to go into greater depth. On the other hand, they may require a response, question or encouragement to continue. Trust yourself to know when to speak and when to stay silent.

9. Trust yourself also to ask the right question or to say what is needed at the appropriate time, rather than preparing it as you listen. Often we have heard only a fraction of what is said before mentally preparing our solution. If what you say doesn't seem right, don't panic. Let it go and try something else.

10. Finally, don't become a clone of some technique you have learned. Adapt your style to whatever is or is not working with THIS person NOW. Some need silent listening, some need their words reflected back, some need effective questioning, some need endorsement, some need challenging and some need whatever it is you are going to make up as you go!! Listening is an art more than a science and involves the heart as well as the head.

Apply this to listening to yourself:

Reflection point   **Listening to yourself**

Are you ready to be present, patient and non-judgemental with yourself?

Are you ready to find out who you are, and what is going on with you, rather than what you think should be there?

Are you ready to create time and space to be with yourself, away from outside distractions, and without an agenda?

Are you ready to hear something different today from yesterday as you evolve and change and go deeper into yourself?

Are you ready to give yourself the gift of listening?

Truth telling

In order for you to make conscious, positive changes, you need to tell the truth about what you want to have happen and about what is currently happening. Truth telling is not about looking good or getting gold stars and it can only happen in an atmosphere of acceptance and positive regard. If you judge someone, have lots of pre-conceptions about how they should be, and if you are likely to tell them how awful they generally are, then it is not too likely that they will reveal much of themselves to you. In fact, that would be a pretty silly thing to do!

In the same way, the more that you are ready to accept yourself as you are, the more open and real you can be with yourself. Then you have a foundation for being more effective in whatever it is that you want to do. It is like going on a journey. Suppose I want to go from Inverness to Newcastle but I think it would be more glamorous if I were starting from Paris, so I convince myself that this is where I am! Planning the route and making the bookings is going to be a strange and frustrating experience ... .

The emphasis on dealing with the truth of 'what is' in any situation, rather than with what should be there or what you would like to be there, is fundamental to all coaching interactions. Small businesses frequently fail because the owners think that the public should want what they have to offer, rather than finding out and responding to what the public actually do want. Leaders frequently emphasize how their staff should be motivated, rather than finding out what does motivate them. Relationships go awry when you blinker yourself and see only what you want to see in your partner, rather than responding to how they really are.

Creating visions or goals based on what you should want, or what you think looks good to other people, results in burden and struggle. So whatever you're involved in, a good coach will always encourage you to tell the truth about what you are dealing with and what you want.

Reflection point   Telling the truth

Where do you avoid telling the truth about things?

What is this costing you?

What is the one truth that you would most benefit from taking on board?

What is 'true for you' is an expression of how you see things and what you are about, now. It does not mean that this is, or should, be the 'truth' for somebody else. It may take time and persistence to get to the core of what is really true for you. On top of this, what is true for you will change with time and experience. To listen to yourself is an ongoing process and not something which can be done once, summarized and taken for granted.

Throughout the book so far I have been encouraging you to listen to yourself, particularly through the different reflection points. They all encourage you to go past superficial replies, and ideas of how you should be, and to stand up for what is really true for you – at this time. We will now look together at some other listening areas and approaches.

Different approaches to listening to yourself

When communicating with and finding out about yourself, there are different approaches and methods that you can explore. Some are more left-brain and logical, some are more right-brain and intuitive while some are a combination of the two.

They all involve becoming more present and conscious of what is going on with you. Thinking actively and consciously is a very different experience from being deluged with the automatic, background thoughts that frequently occupy us. In the same way, consciously listening to the nuances of your feelings and inner promptings is very different from being swayed by unconscious emotions and reactions. And talking with awareness and reflection is very different from just churning out your story.

Most people make nowhere near enough time available really to get to know themselves, or consciously to consider their choices and responses to different situations. Pressures and busyness take over and the intention to take some time out can easily get lost. In the thick of the action it can be difficult to get an overview and to make clear decisions about the way forward. That is why, in battle, experienced commanders will sometimes take themselves to a nearby hilltop where they can think clearly, get an overview and plan their campaign before re-joining the troops.

There are two aspects of connecting with yourself to consider:

- Firstly, the practice of quietening down and simply spending quality time with yourself, as you ideally would with a friend or one of your family. Getting to know yourself in depth through reflection, silence, and other non-verbal activity.

- Secondly, when there is a situation that you are involved in or want to make a decision about. Being able to connect fully with your experience, thoughts, intuition and wisdom so as to make your decision from the most informed and resourceful state.

We'll start by considering approaches where you put aside special time to listen to yourself. Later, we'll also look at some ways for connecting and checking-in with yourself that don't take much time and which you can do during the day.

Creating space and quietening down

Many of us live very busy lives, in the course of which we are bombarded with information, ideas and emotional hooks. Even when you are alone, thoughts, messages and emotions from the day can continue to dominate you. They are like static that prevents you from tuning into yourself. In order to be your own person, and to draw on your real power, you need to be able to detach somehow from this background static and allow it to quieten down. As you do this, you strengthen the observer and chooser in you. This is the part of you who is aware of, and appreciates, your thoughts and feelings and yet is separate from them and has a choice in how to deal with them. You have thoughts and feelings, yet you are more than your thoughts and feelings.

As the chooser and authority in your own life, you can learn to acknowledge and listen to the different parts that make up your personality, integrate them and choose the overall direction in which you will go forward. You are like the conductor of an orchestra listening to the different players, cueing some in, quietening others down and integrating them into some kind of harmony. Being able to detach from passing thoughts and feelings and being able to reside more in this aspect of yourself, as the observer and chooser, gives you a great sense of stability and strength. From this place of inner calm, you are far better equipped to travel through the ups and downs of life.

Ways of connecting with this place in yourself, that work for different folk, include meditation, reflection, and a variety of everyday activities and pastimes. Anything that allows you to be more focused in present time, to let go of your busyness and to be less overtaken with regrets about the past or worries about the future, can work.

Meditation

Most meditation practices involve sitting in a balanced and relaxed position and gently focusing your attention on something in present time – whether it is the sensation of your breath entering and leaving your nostrils, a word or sound, or perhaps a picture of some kind. As thoughts and emotions come and go, you notice them and gently bring your focus back to your chosen object of attention. Through practice, your ability to stay centred and not to be taken over by thoughts and emotions gets stronger. Other benefits include relaxation and, occasionally, insights that come from a deeper place of knowing. There are numerous books and courses available on meditation. Some are aligned with a particular spiritual perspective while others are more purely practical in nature. *The Relaxation Response,* by Dr Herbert Benson (Avon Books, 2000), takes the latter approach.

Here is one simple meditation practice you can try, based on being aware of your breathing. Start by sitting comfortably, with your arms and legs uncrossed, and your back gently upright without straining. You can sit on cushions or on a chair – whichever suits you. If you use a chair, have both feet flat on the floor and rest your hands on your thighs or in your lap. If possible, set a timer for 20 minutes, or whatever time you decide to give it, so that you don't need to keep looking at the clock. Now close your eyes and simply notice the sensation of the breath going in and out of your nostrils. Don't try and control the breathing in any way. Just follow it. If you realize that your attention has been taken over by other things, don't make a big deal about it or give yourself a hard time – and don't try to fight the thoughts or stop them. Simply acknowledge that your attention has wandered and bring it back to noticing the flow of breath. At first, it is very common for your attention to wander a lot of the time, but with practice you will find it easier to stay focused.

Connecting with yourself through an activity

If meditation doesn't do it for you then there are lots of other approaches. Connecting with yourself does not have to involve some special or esoteric discipline. Any simple activity can become a kind of meditation practice, if you keep bringing your attention back to your experience in the present time. I used to enjoy running outdoors, being aware of my breathing and the rhythm and sound of my feet touching the ground. Walking in nature, while hearing the sounds and seeing the things around me is similar. I have had clients who found that they were most present and relaxed while doing the ironing. Others find that painting and drawing or listening with full attention to music they love has the same effect.

What you do is not as important as how you do it. For you, it might be gardening, exercise, sewing, taking a leisurely bath, or any activity that you enjoy and which allows you to become present, to let go of the swirl of ongoing concerns and to tune into yourself. If you already have something that works well for you, choose to do it regularly. Schedule it in before everything else, rather than hoping that it will happen and knowing that most times it won't! If you don't already have something that works for you, choose something from the ideas in this chapter to start with. Again, schedule regular times for it before filling your diary.

There are also numerous relaxation tapes and CDs available to help you quieten down and connect with yourself. If you use one regularly, you will find that you don't need to focus so much on the words and can simply sink down inside yourself. One that I have produced is *Coming Home to You,* based on the Alexander Technique. (This is available at the members' section at www.self-factor.com.)

Reflection point   **Ways that work for you**

What has worked best for you, in the past, to quieten down and to connect with yourself?

What other methods might you like to explore?

What will you choose to do in the next month?

Clarifying situations and making choices

There will be many times when you will want to get clearer about what is going on and how you feel about a particular situation. You will also want to clarify what outcome you want and what you need to do about it. Because people can have very different styles of accessing and processing information, there are lots of different approaches to getting clearer. To give you a sense of what is possible, I have listed a wide variety of them here, including a few that are a bit more unusual. You can browse through them, try some out and discover what works for you. You may find, as I do, that what works for you one day may not serve you so well another day. So stay flexible.

The most common approaches involve some form of verbalization, either as the main factor or alongside other techniques. There are also a number of non-verbal approaches which connect with your intuition and wisdom and provide alternative or additional information. It can be good to consider things on your own and it can also be helpful to have somebody else as a support, catalyst or sounding board.

Verbal approaches (internal or spoken)

Quality thinking time

Simply taking time to think things through for yourself, away from other pressures and distractions, can be enormously helpful, provided that you are really thinking and not just rehashing old thoughts and ideas. Many times our thinking is distracted by outside interruptions or else we go off on a tangent about something that we have remembered we need to do later. Most thinking can be helped by writing down questions, ideas, options and decisions. Here are a few tips for making your reflection time more productive:

- Put aside a definite time when you will not be disturbed
- Put your answer machine on and don't take any phone calls
- Keep a note pad handy to jot down any reminders for yourself
- Ask yourself what you want to come out of the session and write it down
- Ask yourself the three key questions:
  - What is really true for you?
  - What do you really want?
  - What is the best way forward for you?

If you find that your thinking still wanders around and you are just going through the motions, or else that you are worrying rather than thinking constructively, try the following exercise for which you take ONLY ten minutes to start with.

Power thinking

- Think of an issue that has been concerning you.
  - e.g. The poor communication in your team at work.
- Write your concern down as a question.
  - e.g. 'How can I improve communication in my team?'
- Spend five minutes thinking of nothing but how to answer this

question. If you find your mind wandering, bring it back to considering the question. During these five minutes, don't write anything down or do anything else.

- After five minutes, spend a further five minutes writing down legibly what occurred to you, and adding to it.
- After the ten minutes, act on the ideas that you have come up with or get on with whatever else needs doing, but don't re-cycle around the same concern.

The idea of this approach is to focus your mind sharply and constructively rather than worrying ineffectively about something. Once you get used to thinking in this focused way, you may be able to sustain it for longer periods, as happens in a coaching session.

Walk and talk

Another interesting variation on thinking things through comes from a client of mine, called Andrew. He calls it 'walk and talk'.

CASE STUDY ~ ANDREW

Andrew is a highly-qualified corporate accountant who does contract work, operating as departmental head. When he is faced with a decision, Andrew walks up and down his apartment while discussing issues out loud with himself. He finds that hearing the words spoken, and the different nuances in his own voice, gives him more information and frees up his mind far more than just silently thinking. He also complements this with writing things down and summarizing ideas. Andrew pointed out that using the 'walk and talk' technique is not a good idea if you work in an open-plan office .... .

Using an outside sounding board

Talking over what you are thinking and feeling with somebody else, whether it is a friend, colleague, coach or counsellor, can be extremely helpful. It can help you get more perspective on your experience and strengthen the observer and chooser in you.

If you talk things through with someone, make sure that you are consciously exploring new possibilities, and not just recycling old stories or venting your feelings in victim mode. Look for people who will give you a safe space to talk and who have a basic trust in your ability to handle things and to find and act on your own solutions. If using a friend or colleague for this purpose, it can help if you set things up explicitly beforehand. Explain that you just want to be listened to and supported in listening to yourself and finding out what is true for you. Let them know that, even if you are facing challenges, you are still okay and don't need them to fix you or to tell you what to do. And then you can do the same for them, another time.

In a coaching situation, you are supported in listening to yourself, and acknowledging what is true for you, in the context of taking responsibility, coming up with your own solutions and moving forward in your life.

Your inner mentor

An alternative slant on thinking and talking things through is to have in mind some kind of inner mentor. This can be a relative, teacher, boss, famous personality or whoever. Think of someone that you respect and hold a conversation with them in your imagination. What would they say was important and what might they advise you to do? The Board of Advisors exercise given below is a structured example of this.

Your board of advisors

Just as an organization will sometimes gather a board of experts, to advise and guide them, so you can have your own, imaginary board of advisors, or Brains Trust. Think of three or more figures whom you admire and whose support and guidance you would appreciate. These can be people that you know or anyone that you have heard of. It can even be an imaginary figure, such as Gandolph, from *Lord of the Rings*. Choose figures with different qualities between them including, but not limited to, clear thinking, wisdom, courage, experience and humour.

Take any situation you want to get clearer on and set no more than three questions to ask each of the members of your board. For instance, supposing that you are concerned about your health, you might pose the following questions:

- What do I most need to understand about my health?
- What change would make the biggest positive difference?
- What is the first thing that I need to do?

Then have an imaginary dialogue with each advisor in turn. You may like to do this sitting quietly with your eyes closed or you may like to walk around and allow yourself to get into the character of each advisor. At the end of your time with each member of your board, thank them for their input and write down their answers. Finally, look at all the answers together and see what is relevant and what you may now want to act on.

Writing your way clear

As part of the different thinking approaches above, writing things down helps to clarify questions and ideas. You can also use writing as the main way of getting clearer on something. Here are a few ideas:

Brainstorming key points and options

Whatever situation you want to get clearer on, it usually helps to write down what the key points are to consider and what your options might be for moving forward. If you find it difficult to get started, you can kick things off with a brainstorming session. Take a blank sheet of foolscap paper and give yourself a limited time, say five minutes. Write down, in any order, anything that comes to mind to do with the situation. Use single words or bullet points, rather than sentences. Don't censor it, try to order it or make sense of it while you are writing. Just get your ideas out and down on paper, writing quickly but legibly. Then take a number of coloured crayons or highlighting pens and use different colours to group together items on the paper that seem to belong together. Finally, assign headings to the different groups and write them out again, under those headings, on a new piece of paper. This can then form the basis for reflection, discussion, planning, making a presentation or whatever.

Another way of recording and further developing the information that comes out of this approach is to use a mind map. This is a visual way of showing the outline of a subject using keywords and arrows. I won't go further into mind maps here but I recommend them and there are a number of good books on using them, including *Present Yourself* (Jalmar Books, 1988) by motivational speaker and Alexander Teacher, Michael J. Gelb.

Journaling

Keeping a journal is a reflective form of writing that can help you to connect with yourself and get an ongoing perspective on what is going on for you. This can be written in depth or it can just consist of jotting down key thoughts, experiences and insights at the end of the day. Some people like to journal about a particular theme or to focus on a certain area. An example of this is to keep a gratitude journal where you list all the things that you are grateful for in your life and day. This can be enormously uplifting and puts the negative experiences in perspective amongst all the good that happens. Keep a gratitude journal for a month and see how your perspective and outlook change.

Free writing

This is a method for bypassing 'shoulds' and judgements as you listen to yourself and access your thoughts, feelings and wisdom. You write freehand continuously, without planning, ordering or censoring what comes out. Write without undue pausing and let yourself change direction randomly, or stay on one topic – whatever occurs for you. It does not have to make sense or be nice or reasonable. You just write. Some people like to keep the pages and read them over later while my preference is to scrap them and let them go. When I write quickly I cannot read them anyway! I trust that what is important to me will stay with me. Later, you can organize, reflect on it and write out key points if you want to. That is a different kind of writing.

I find that anything between 1 and 3 pages of foolscap works for me, and that the best time is first thing in the morning. For you it may be different. If I am feeling particularly confused or troubled, I commit to at least 3 pages of free writing and then just go for it. I nearly always feel lighter afterwards. As with all techniques, you need to try it a few times to find out if it is going to work for you but this has been a favourite for me and many of my clients.

Letters for your eyes only ...

Writing a letter, in the knowledge that no one else is going to read it, can be enormously liberating as a way to find out what you really think, feel and want. There are three types that you may use:

- Letters to someone that you have issues or uncertainties about
- Letters to someone that you consider to be a wise advisor
- Letters to yourself

Suppose that you have a sense of unease or grievance with a personal or business acquaintance and it keeps nagging away at you. You can't let it go and yet you don't feel clear enough, or else you don't feel it is appropriate, to talk with them about it. Write them a letter, knowing beforehand that you are not going to send it. Pull out all the stops, hold nothing back and tell them exactly what you have to say to them. Don't worry about taking responsibility or whether it is true or not. Just keep writing until you feel a bit clearer. Then destroy the letter. Afterwards you can decide what, if anything, you want to do about the situation, including speaking to the person or writing another letter that you *will* send. But, in the first instance, the letter is for your eyes only.

Writing to a wise advisor is a variation on dialoguing with a mentor in your imagination. It can be to a specific, imagined person or it can be to your wise, inner self. Write to them, explaining the situation and your concerns, as fully as possible and asking for their advice. Take a break and then, some time later, read the letter, as if you were the wise advisor reading it for the first time. Then, from the point of view of the advisor, write a letter back to yourself giving your viewpoint and advice.

Another variation on writing to yourself is to send an encouraging letter to yourself, to be kept and opened in time of need. We all have our ups and downs when we feel more or less resourceful. When you are in a particularly good space, write a letter acknowledging and encouraging yourself and putting down on paper what you would like to remember the next time you are going through a tough time. It could be soft and reassuring or it could be more determined and kick arse with compassion.

Metaphor

Metaphors interweave with how you experience and approach life. They also give another way of accessing knowledge and wisdom through words, whether spoken or written. You will find that some metaphors are already being emphasized in your life or business and that you can then consciously explore and play with them. You can also choose to create and emphasize new metaphors that open things up for you.

Suppose that you are developing a business and are considering how to increase your market share. One common metaphor might be that of going to war and needing to get the troops mobilized. This metaphor brings a sense of urgency and possible danger and emphasizes the need to defeat the opposition. As an alternative, you could see yourself, and your products, as providing customers with a much needed, but relatively unknown, source of nutrients. Then you might place more emphasis on forming relationships, gaining trust with customers, educating them on their needs and providing reliable service. Neither metaphor is the 'correct' one to use but whichever one you emphasize will affect how you think and what you do. So it makes sense to be more conscious about the metaphors you choose to use.

Another common metaphor, applicable to many situations, is that of going on a journey. As an example, think of a relationship that you are currently involved in, whether personal or business. Let your imagination roam as you play with the following questions. Imagine that your relationship is like some kind of shared journey:

- *Who is deciding the destination?*
- *Are you walking, driving or using some other form of transport?*
- *What are the weather and other conditions like?*
- *What would make the journey more comfortable?*
- *Where would be the best destination to aim for?*
- *How could you get there more quickly?*
- *How long do you want to travel together?*

Now, de-brief and see if your answers to these questions give you any new ideas on your relationship.

Storytelling

Stories and parables, like metaphors, can connect deeply with people and give them new ways of looking at their own lives. Many spiritual teachers and other leaders have used them in this way. It can be very empowering to collect stories and examples, whether real or fictional, that inspire you and others.

You can also use your imagination to make up your own stories, to throw light on a particular situation. This is an approach that I came across and loved many years ago, during a communications training. It is not to everyone's taste but can be great fun, particularly if done with a friend or colleague over a coffee or a glass of wine. One of you explains the situation that you want to get clearer on. Then the other one simply trusts their intuition to come up with some ideas and insights, in the form of a story. The following words are a good way to start and then you simply roll with it: 'Here is a story which I think might throw some light on your situation. Once upon a time there was ...' If you are the storyteller, don't try and plan it out. Just see where it goes and where it ends up. I have had great fun and some great insights with this. If you would like to give it a go, try it with someone with whom you don't feel under pressure and where it doesn't matter if the story flops.

Other, non-verbal approaches

Metaphor, storytelling, and some of the other approaches so far, draw on different ways of experiencing and knowing than come from purely logical sources. There are many non-verbal methods that draw on both common sense and these other sources of intuitive understanding and wisdom.

Some people dismiss intuitive approaches out of hand. I have studied logic twice, firstly as part of my Mathematics degree and secondly as part of a Philosophy course. My view is that a truly logical mind has no problem with accepting and working alongside processes that are intuitive and hence not logical. It neither rejects intuition nor puts it on a pedestal. It is the pseudo-logical mind that denies its limitations, tries to control everything and is afraid, or dismissive, of intuitive and other ways of knowing things. There is, though, a need for discernment.

The need for both openness and discernment

Your intuitions about things are not infallible and need to be considered both respectfully and with discernment. The challenge is that, outside your conscious thinking and awareness, you have at least three factors that may be influencing you:

- common sense picking up on non-verbal clues
- unconscious, mindless programming
- deep inner wisdom

Hence, when you access ideas from your unconscious mind, don't dismiss them off hand – likewise, don't assume that they must be right. Treat them with discernment. Here are a few further ideas for clarifying a situation or making a decision, that may connect with you.

Accessing body wisdom

The practice of checking in with your body sensations to make a decision is one of the most direct ways to access your intuition. Two of the most effective questions to ask are:

- What is your gut feeling about this?
- What does your heart tell you to do?

Most of us have some 'sense' that we feel somewhere in our body when something is right for us. You may find that you can rely on this sense of 'rightness' more than on words and logic when the chips are down. This is partly because your body instinct is less accessible to manipulation by 'shoulds' and outside influences.

Take a few moments now to become more conscious of how you intuitively know when something is right or not.

Reflection point   **Knowing something is right**

Remember a time when you just 'knew' that something was right.

How did it feel and where in your body did you feel it?

Now remember a time when you had a bad feeling about something or someone and 'knew' that something wasn't right for you.

How did that feel and where did you feel it?

For many people, the feeling of something's being right is somehow freer and more expansive. In contrast, the feeling that something is wrong is tighter and more contracting. Listening to your body wisdom does not guarantee that you will always be right and there is a need to use discernment and to balance it with clear thinking. On the other hand, ignoring or suppressing your body wisdom means ignoring additional information that comes from both common sense and inner knowing.

How often have you had an intuition, not listened to it and subsequently regretted it? On the other hand, how often have you followed your intuition and wished that you hadn't? When I ask these questions, of coaches in training, the answers lean heavily towards wishing that they had listened to and followed their intuition more. As you become more tuned into your own, internal sense of when something is right for you or not, you can pause at any time and check out your gut instinct or what you know in your heart.

Holding a question

You can adapt many of the activities given earlier in the chapter (for quietening down and connecting with yourself) to help you reflect on a particular area of your life or to make a decision. You simply pose a question to yourself, before and during the activity, with the intention of becoming clearer. For instance, if you're having problems with a department at work, then you may pose the question, 'What do I need to understand about myself and this department?' before meditating, exercising or doing whatever it is that you do. Simply hold the question, notice any words, pictures or other insights that occur to you but don't try to force anything. Keep your main focus on the activity. If something relevant to your question occurs, fine — and if not, fine. Relax anyway and the question will continue to reside in your unconscious and may be answered at a later time.

PERSONAL CASE STUDY ~ HOLDING A QUESTION

I had been thinking through and writing, over a week or so, how I wanted to tackle values in this chapter. Holding this as a question, one morning, a completely fresh and better idea presented itself during a 20 minute meditation.

Maintaining an inquiry

In order to find out the truth about things, it doesn't always work to go with the first answer that you come up with. Sometimes it takes more soul-searching and ongoing inquiry. One way to do this is to pose the question, write it down and reflect upon it every day for a week or so. For example, you might ask yourself, 'What would it take for me really to enjoy my work?' Mull it over, maybe talk about it with friends or colleagues. Notice headlines in the paper, images in magazines or on TV, phrases from songs or adverts — anything that connects with you and your inquiry. Keep a small notebook with you and keep returning to the question. Write down anything that resonates or occurs to you. You can do this with any of the questions from the reflection points that seem important for you.

CASE STUDY ~ DOROTHY

Dorothy was a counsellor in training, who also ran her own small business and worked with the local social services at their youth centre. They asked her to take on the management of the centre full time and she was considering what to do. Rather than limiting herself to accepting or declining their offer, I suggested that she held her own inquiry around the question, 'What would it take for me really to enjoy my work?' – and then to be pro-active in going for what she wanted. After staying with the question for a while she realized that she wanted part time work and that it needed to have an emphasis on counselling the young people. She approached the organization with this and they agreed with both parts of the request, with the proviso that the counselling would have to come from their next budget period. She has taken the job, really enjoys it as it is, and is moving towards setting up a new counselling service.

Intuition and relationships

It is said that less than 10% of communication is verbal. This means that you are constantly picking up from other people clues that you may not consciously be aware of. When you use your intuition to help you understand and improve relationships, you are drawing on all of the information available, including your own understanding and wisdom. Effective communicators rely heavily on their imagination and intuition, whether they realize it or not. They possess the ability to 'put themselves in the other's shoes', to 'look at things from a different perspective' and to 'take an outside view'.

Here are a few ways in which you can develop and use these abilities. Think of someone with whom you would like to improve your relationship, and remember a specific time when you were talking with them. Then:

- Put yourself in their shoes and imagine that you are them, talking with you. Feel what it is like to be them and, as them, ask yourself these questions:
  - What am I thinking?
  - What am I feeling?
  - What do I want?
- Now imagine that you are your own wise self, watching yourself as you are talking with this other person:
  - What do you notice about yourself and how you are being?
  - What are you doing that gets in the way of good communication?
  - How could you improve your communication?
- Now imagine that you are an outside observer, watching the two of you together:
  - What is the dynamic between these two people?
  - What needs to change or happen for them to move forward?

Armed with any new information that comes out of these exercises, how can you now interact with this person more happily and effectively? If, as often happens when doing these exercises, you realize that you have not been acting as well as you might, don't be hard on yourself. Appreciate yourself for being willing to look at things and then set about improving your side of the communication.

I have used an extended form of these exercises with a team of corporate accountants, who are not generally thought of as being able or willing to step outside the box. Yet every one of them was amazed at how much information they were able to access and subsequently act upon.

About imagery

There are many different ways in which to work with imagination and images. One common misunderstanding is that you have to be good at seeing pictures in your imagination for imagery to work for you. Not having a strong visual sense myself, I used to get hung up on this before I realized that using your imagination works whatever sensory systems are being utilized when you think of something. For instance, imagine now that you have a large apple in your hand. Have a look at it and take a bite. What colour is it? Is it soft or crunchy? Now throw it in the bin. What sound does it make as it lands in the bin? Just give the first answers that come to you. In other words, just make it up. That is what using your imagination means – making stuff up. If you can come up with answers to those questions, you can use image-work.

Guided imagery

Guided imagery, or visualizations as they are usually called, are where someone else talks you through an experience in your imagination. This allows you to focus on your experience without having to remember what to do next. A frequent assumption about using imagery in this way is that it has to take a long time. When I first started leading telephone conference calls, for coaches in training, I experimented with leading guided visualizations and making them much shorter than I had done previously with groups. Including an initial relaxation phase, I found that we could often gain significant benefits in ten minutes or less. A number of sample guided imageries are available for you to listen to on-line at the members' section of the web site www.self-factor.com.

Using imagery to solve problems

The use of imagery to solve problems involves representing a challenge in another medium. You explore the situation and generate fresh options, in the new medium, and finally de-brief by translating the experiences gained back into words relevant to the original challenge. There are analogies to this process in the world of Mathematics. For instance, a 'real-life' problem involving objects and forces can be represented in Applied Mathematics by vectors and solved with analysis and/or scale drawing. The solution arrived at can then be translated back and expressed in the language of objects and forces. Some of the most elegant mathematical proofs and solutions use this kind of approach.

Using an image as a metaphor

You can use an image to provide a metaphor for your life, or for a particular situation that you want to get clear on. The idea is that you phrase your concern as a question for your unconscious mind to help you with. In the world of imagery there are no restrictions on what can happen or on how an object can be transformed. You simply let your unconscious imagination do its thing and then see whether or not it makes any useful sense to you later on.

Here is a simple example where you let an organic, everyday object – such as a flower, fruit or vegetable – represent a situation on which you want clarity. At each stage you ask a question and then go with the first response that comes, even if it doesn't seem to make any sense at the time. The stages used below are ones that you can use each time and the examples given are an amalgam based on images that clients have come up with.

- Phrase your concern as a question.
  - e.g. 'How can I best develop my career?'
- Take the first image that comes to mind.
  - e.g. A yellow rose.
- Notice as much as you can about the object, including its condition, location and the surroundings.
  - e.g. The rose is wilting, in a small pot on a wooden table in the corner of a dimly lit room.
- Thank your unconscious and ask it: 'What is the essence of this image?'
  - e.g. Dying from being in the wrong conditions.

- Thank your unconscious and ask it: 'What is the history of this image?'
  - e.g. When the rose was first bought it was smaller and fitted the pot. It was near a window and healthy. As it grew, it became too big for the pot and no longer gets enough water. It has also been moved to a back room with less light. It feels unnoticed and unappreciated.
- Thank your unconscious and ask it: 'What are the worst and best case scenarios?'
  - e.g. Worst case: the rose stays where it is and gets droopier and droopier until it dies for lack of light and water.
  - e.g. Best case: the rose moves and grows and blooms.
- Thank your unconscious and ask it: 'What is the best way forward?'
  - e.g. The rose rises in the air from the pot and out of the window. It goes through the window of another, nearby building which is light and airy and sees that there is a large pot waiting by a window. The rose gently settles in here and immediately starts to prosper. Passers by comment on how beautiful it is and how fragrant the perfume.
- Thank your unconscious and spend a few minutes seeing what analogies there are with you real life concern and how you might use the information that you have gained.
  - e.g. You realize that you have outgrown your job and no longer get the support and input that used to nourish you. You used to liaise directly with clients (the open window) and have since been promoted to a backroom managerial role that doesn't satisfy your need to get out there more and be hands-on. You realize that if you stay where you are it can only get worse. The solution is not just to move within the same company but to change companies (i.e. changing buildings in the image) where you have the space and support to take on a bigger role with more contact with clients. You want to move somewhere where you are more appreciated.

I have used this basic technique successfully to throw light and generate new ideas on a wide variety of situations. As with all the other methods on offer here, try it out and see whether it suits you. If not, use something else. An excellent book on using imagery is *Life Choices, Life Changes: Develop Your Personal Vision for the Life you Want* (Hodder Mobius, London, 2003) by Dina Glouberman. The above technique is adapted from her Image as Life Metaphor exercise.

Getting inspiration from the arts

Good literature abounds with examples of characters and situations from which you can draw inspiration. The same is true of poetry, theatre, music and dance. The poet and speaker, David Whyte, author of *The Heart Aroused: Poetry and the Presence of the Soul at Work* (Spiro Press, 1996), is in great demand in the corporate world. He gives inspired, key note speeches and seminars where he uses poetry to inform, motivate and develop leadership and vision. Benjamin Zander, conductor of the Boston Philharmonic Orchestra, is another inspirational speaker and seminar leader in great demand. He co-authored with his wife, Rosamund Stone Zander, *The Art of Possibility: Transforming Professional and Personal Life* (Harvard Business School Press, 2000). He uses his experience of conducting an orchestra to teach about and encourage positive approaches to life, work and leadership. You can also gain understanding and clarity by expressing yourself in different artistic ways, without having to be 'good' at them.

Using drawing and painting

As with the use of storytelling, the idea here is to have a question in mind and then to just start drawing or painting whatever comes to you without thinking about it, censoring or trying to make sense of it. Once you've finished you can reflect on what you have expressed and see if it shines any light on your concern.

A variation on this is to create a collage. Have a collection of magazines with lots of pictures, a large piece of card or paper (blank wallpaper works well), scissors, a glue stick and some felt-tip pens. Set yourself a focus question, such as 'What would my ideal life look like?' Then give yourself a limited amount of time, say 30–40 minutes. Cut out any pictures that appeal and stick them on the card. You can also draw or write words on the card. At the end, take some time to reflect on what images are represented and what they mean for you. If the collage is meaningful for you, keep it and stick it up somewhere you can see it and reflect on it.

You can use virtually any form of artistic expression to help you clarify a situation or to make a decision. As an example, here is a more unusual one:

Movement and dance

In my role of Alexander teacher, I sometimes used to co-lead movement workshops with an inspired dancer and therapist, Sharon Took-Zozayer, and a brilliant musician, Philip Stuart. I would start a session with some movement and relaxation, to help participants become more centred and connected with their body. Sharon would then take them through guided movements where they explored different themes. Philip tuned into what was happening and provided impromptu accompaniment with percussion and instruments. Having lead my section, I would often join in as a participant. I remember one exercise where we were asked to choose a situation in which we wanted to make changes.

PERSONAL CASE STUDY ~ USING MOVEMENT

I focused on one of my work relationships that felt stuck and negative. Sharon first asked us to create a dance, or movement sequence, that reflected the current situation. My movements were sluggish, tight and constrained, taking very little physical space and with my body held in and slumped. We were then asked to move to a different location in the room and to create a dance that expressed how we would like things to be. This time my movement was free and expansive, travelling through a lot of space, with my body feeling open and fluid. Finally, we were asked to go back to the original location and, starting with the first movement sequence, to dance out the transition until we arrived at the new location with the new movement. Although my normal tendency might have been to do something dramatic, this time I approached it very tentatively. I moved slowly, trying things out. I moved forward, then back a little until it felt safe to move out further. Bit by bit, my body and my movement opened out until I was finally moving freely in the new location. Afterwards, in the de-briefing stage, I realized that, given the personalities involved, the relationship would not improve with confrontation or any attempt on my part to force things along. The best strategy was to make small overtures and test the waters until we could feel more at ease together and communication could flow. And this was what worked in practice.

I have included a wide variety of alternative methods, so that you realize that there are many ways of tapping into your intuition and finding ways forward. While helpful for some people, they are not obligatory so don't feel that you have to use them. Allow yourself to experiment and then decide what approaches really work best for you. This could be one of the more intuitive methods or it could be simply sitting down and thinking things through, with a pen and paper.

However you approach it, as we said earlier, the bottom line is to go beyond superficial responses and to find your own authentic answers to the questions:

- What is really true for you?
- What do you really want?
- What is the best way forward?

Feelings

One area that can be tricky for many people is how to listen to and relate to their feelings. Feelings are natural and part of the ongoing process of being alive and being touched by different experiences. They are part of what makes you human and they contain energy. Without feelings, your life would be a dull, grey and soulless place. Yet *with* feelings it can be more changeable and potentially chaotic than you may want to deal with.

Dealing with feelings

In order to operate well with your feelings, here are a few skills which are helpful:

- Firstly, to realize that you have feelings and yet are more than your feelings alone. This allows you to acknowledge and listen to your feelings yet still to have a choice over whether or not to act on them.
- Secondly, you want to be able to express your feelings effectively and appropriately when it serves you.
- Thirdly, you want to be able to acknowledge your feelings and put them to one side when that is what serves you best. You want to have feelings and yet not be run by your feelings.

When you are able to access your feelings, without being taken over by them, you can continue to listen to yourself and frequently go to another level of subtler feeling and knowing.

For instance, you may feel scared at the prospect of doing something new or different. Yet if you dig down deeper you may 'feel' or 'know' that it is the right thing for you to do – or not. The first level of emotional reaction is valid and human and needs to be acknowledged. Then you can access your deeper wisdom. If you try to deny or fight with your emotional reactions, you will get rigid and will not be able to reach this other level of knowing. Equally, if you think that your feelings always have to take centre stage, you will become an emotional danger zone and will also be unable to access your deeper wisdom and resources.

Reflection point   **Dealing with your feelings**

How at ease are you with acknowledging and expressing your feelings?

Can you access your deeper wisdom beneath the emotional reactions?

Can you express your feelings and ask for what you want, when appropriate?

When appropriate, can you put your feelings to one side and choose to do what is right for you?

If you find it difficult to access and feel your feelings, or else you find yourself frequently overwhelmed and run by feelings, it can be very helpful to work with a good counsellor or therapist. Accessing and dealing with powerful emotions is not the remit of the coaching process.

What we can look at are ways of being with the everyday feelings that are a part of life. The core of emotional intelligence is being aware of your feelings and then being able to manage them appropriately and effectively.

The language of emotions

How you speak about emotions has a big impact, both on how aware of them you are and on how you are able to manage them. When discerning how you feel, it helps if you have a range of possibilities to consider rather than labelling everything as either good or bad. Start by taking a brief emotional survey of how you feel about the different areas of your life, at this time. Jot down some answers.

Reflection point **How do you feel?**

What do you feel glad about in your life?

What do you feel mad about in your life?

What do you feel sad about in your life?

This is just a handy shorthand to get you started. Now enlarge on some of the things you have noted by asking yourself, 'What kind of glad/mad/said is it that I feel?' For instance, if you realized that you feel glad about an evening out with somebody, then ask yourself, 'What kind of glad do I feel?' It might be amused, relieved, tender, excited, mellow, curious, expectant, exuberant, cheerful, grateful, or whatever else comes to mind. If you said that you felt mad about how a meeting went, ask yourself, 'What kind of mad do I feel?' It might be agitated, frustrated, vengeful, irked, antagonistic, misunderstood, thwarted, disrespected, aloof, or whatever. If you feel sad about how the weekend went with the family, then ask yourself, 'What kind of sad?' This could include troubled, disappointed, discouraged, tearful, guilty, rejected, or whatever.

As you become more familiar with the nuances of your feelings, you can just ask yourself directly and simply, 'What am I really feeling about this?' The answer will give you more clarity on what is happening and what, if anything, you want to do about it. This could include changing your behaviour, getting some needs met or making requests of other people. It can also flag up when some old pattern, which is not relevant to the current situation, has been triggered. This can save you from acting out, making things worse and feeling bad about yourself.

This process of becoming curious about and describing your inner landscape, without getting lost in it, also strengthens your sense of being the observer and chooser in your life.

Choosing how you emphasize your feeling

Your choice of language surrounding feelings also reflects what you emphasize and influences how you will experience it. Perversely, many people use language that highlights their negative feelings on the one hand and diminishes their positive feelings on the other. You can choose to do this in reverse without getting unreal or being in denial.

If your cappuccino is a bit cold, you might be a little disgruntled but do you really have to feel 'devastated'? When reflecting on a presentation you gave that got a lukewarm reception, does it really help to call it 'awful' or to say that they 'hated' it? You could just acknowledge that it was weak in places and that you can improve on it.

Or, the other way around, if you are enjoying yourself and someone asks how you feel, you could risk saying and meaning 'I feel excited', rather than saying 'not bad'. Of course, there are cultural differences to be taken into account and what goes down well in the U.S. doesn't always work in Europe, and certainly not in the North of Scotland. A friend of mine, from Aberdeen, describes how when his team scores at football there are no wild cheers from the home crowd – just a few mumbled versions of 'ay, no bad', accompanied by the satisfying rustle of sweetie papers being opened in celebration … .

For the next month, pay attention to the language you use to describe your experiences and feelings. Experiment with making it more positive. Choose to use language that, while still realistic for you, keeps your negative experiences in perspective and emphasizes your positive experiences. Who knows, by the end of the month you might even be acknowledging occasional euphoria …

Values

A powerful tool for listening to yourself, and for making decisions that fit more fully with your own truth and wishes, is to clarify and draw upon your values.

Ways of looking at values

As with many terms in the personal development and business worlds, 'values' is used to mean different things by different authors and practitioners. There is no one 'correct' definition, so it will help if I clarify things a little and say how I approach values.

Relevant definitions of 'value', as a noun, include:

- Worth, importance or desirability
- Moral principle
- Something (as a principle or quality) intrinsically valuable or desirable

The first definition links with thinking of values as simply describing how you currently place importance and priority in your life.

The second definition links with thinking of values as how you should be and do things or how you aspire to be.

The third definition links them to what is an intrinsic expression of the 'real' you and what brings you fulfilment.

Depending on the context and source, you will find one meaning or another being emphasized and they can also cross over. So you get values as:

VALUES IN CONTEXT	Current Situation	'Should'/Aspiration	True Expression
Individual	Habits What you currently make most important.	What you think your values should be. What you aspire to.	An expression of the essential YOU. What is really important to you and brings fulfilment.
Organisation/ Group	Culture. How they do things. What they currently make most important.	What they think their values should be.	A synergy of individual values.

In our work together, I shall primarily be emphasizing the third meaning.

Flower analogy

Imagine that we are different flowers. Perhaps you are a rose and I am bluebell. Our needs are the conditions that enable us to survive and grow and to be healthy plants. We have some needs in common, such as water and light. We have some needs that vary, such as how much light or shade, what kind of soil and how much moisture. If our needs are not met, we become a droopy or a dead plant. And yet the needs are not what we are really about and what we have to offer the world.

Our values, as I use the term, are the natural expression of being the particular flower that we are. While we have some shared values or principles – such as growing and blooming – our personal values might be our particular foliage, blossom and fragrance. In other words, the things which make us unique, bring us fulfilment and are our special contribution to the world. A bluebell trying to be a rose is going to be a sad plant, however well you take care of it!

So, in looking at your values, you are clarifying what is a true expression of who you are, what is essential to you and what brings you fulfilment. Your values are the things you are naturally drawn to rather than what you have to force yourself to do.

Here is another analogy from my work as an Alexander teacher, which involves helping people to live in a more body-friendly way. I support clients as they re-learn to align with their natural poise and movement. My best examples of good movement are healthy 3-year-olds who move with natural grace and balance. They are beautifully aligned and co-ordinated, without the tension that we become used to as adults. Then, over time, and with the pressures of life, most of us develop habits of tension and distortion that cover up and interfere with our natural grace. We slump and twist ourselves and develop our own ways of coping with life that sap energy and effectiveness. In an effort to counteract our habits, we may then force ourselves to sit and stand more upright. While the intention is commendable, the result of this approach is usually stiffness and rigidity because we are attempting to use our willpower and voluntary muscles to hold a position and force ourselves to do the 'right' thing. Real poise comes from releasing the habits of tension and trusting our innate, postural reflexes to guide us.

In a similar way, unmet needs, stress and the 'shoulds' that you take on from others, cover up and make it hard to be in touch with your essential nature and values. They become your habitual ways of living and are like the static on a radio that prevents you from getting a clear signal. Trying to remedy this by forcing yourself to live according to external principles and values is hard work, and also causes physical and emotional rigidity. As you take better care of yourself, get your needs met, eliminate energy drains and let go of 'shoulds', you will find it easier to listen to and to express your true values.

Clarifying values

Sometimes when people want to clarify their values, they start with a list of words to choose from, pick some and then list them in order of priority. While this can be a good kick-start, if that is all you do then it is relatively meaningless and just becomes a list of words that you stick in a file somewhere and bring out on demand. It can also lead you to go 'shopping' for values that sound good and which you think will impress other people. It is similar to the mandatory company mission statement that sits on a side wall in the reception area; it doesn't actually make any difference to your life and how you live it.

The process of coming up with a list of values is what is really important: engaging deeply with and listening to yourself; finding out what is really true for you, what is an expression of the essential you and what brings you fulfilment. Then, out of that process, you may come up with some words or phrases that remind you to connect with and be true to yourself. They are like fingers pointing at the moon; they are very helpful but don't get too caught up with the fingers. Instead, use them to remind you to look at the moon and to be guided by its light.

You do not have to have a list of values written out in order to be true to yourself and to be fulfilled. Living your values is what it is really about. However, if you are able to articulate them, this can be very helpful in steering your way forward and in making decisions. And it is particularly important for leaders that their constituents know what they care about and stand for.

Let's start with your asking yourself some helpful questions and jotting down your responses.

Reflection point   **What are you really about?**

What is really important to you in life?

What is the essence of who you really are and what you are really about?

What are you involved in, and how are you being, when you are most fulfilled?

If all your different needs were fully met, what would still energize you and get you up in the morning?

You can write down single words, phrases or groups of words – whatever seems to encapsulate what you are really about, what is an expression of the real you and what fulfils you. So, your initial list might include things like:

Love
Integrity/truth-telling/doing what is 'right'
Playing music and composing
Being in nature
Synergy and teamwork
Fun and laughter
Intimacy/closeness/tenderness
Making a positive difference in people's lives
Creativity
Connecting deeply with others
Family
Supporting justice and equality
Clarity and communication
Making a meaningful contribution to the world

Clusters of words can be helpful in fleshing out what you really care about. For instance, two people might both have a value of creativity. One might use the cluster of creativity/artistic expression/performance. Another might come up with creativity/innovation/finding new ways of doing things. Creativity is a value for both of them but, when they are fleshed out, you get a better sense of who the person is and what is important to them.

Think about these questions as you go about your daily life. Have conversations with friends, family and colleagues and get their perspective. Support each other in getting clearer about your values.

Another way to connect with your values is to reflect on times in your life when you have felt most alive, fulfilled and truly yourself. Then ask yourself what values were being expressed.

Reflection point **Special times in your life**

What was a special time when you felt really alive and true to yourself?

What were you doing and how were you being?

Who and what else was involved?

What values, important to you, were being expressed at that time?

As you reflect on your values, over a period of time, write them down as key words, phrases or clusters of words. Keep returning to and updating your list until you feel that the values are a good representation of who you are, what you find most important and what brings you fulfilment. Keep the list reasonably short, say between six and ten core values, so that the essence of it is crystallized and you can refer to it as you make plans and decisions.

Honouring your values

Once you have a list of values that are really alive and have meaning for you, then you can look at them and see how much or how little they are currently being honoured in your life. Hence you can then start to make choices that more fully reflect them. Here is a process that you can apply to one or more of your values.

Reflection point **Honouring your values**

Choose one of your core values to consider.

How do you feel when you are really living in accordance with this value?

How do you feel when you are not living in accordance with this value?

Where in your life is this value currently being honoured and expressed?

Where in your life is this value currently being ignored or disrespected?

What would need to change for you to live in full alignment with this value?

What will you commit to doing as a first step to creating this change?

Applying values to decision making

When you have a decision to make, especially a big one involving a possible change of life direction, it can be very helpful to consider your different options in the light of how they do or do not align with your values.

CASE STUDY ~ AILEEN

Aileen was a life and business coach who, after 8 years of marriage, had been through a 6-months trial separation initiated by her husband. They had no children. In contrast to the early years of their relationship, she felt that her husband had become almost entirely work-dominated and was very critical of Aileen if she seemed to slack in his eyes. Her old pattern had been to be the conciliatory one trying to save the relationship and to make things work, even when it meant sacrificing her own interests. In preparation for discussing the future of her marriage, she invested time in getting to know herself more fully, including clarifying her values. This is what she came up with:

- A life of lightness, fun and interaction
- Fully accepting and loving myself and others
- Living authentically – just to be me, no matter what
- Simplifying – cutting out the crap
- Learning the lessons I need to learn – (preferably only once)
- Persevering – getting back up again, even when it is difficult
- Supporting individuals – to grow and lead truly fulfilling lives, whatever that may mean to them
- Appreciating the opportunities in each day
- New things – challenging/being challenged, risk and opportunities

Seeing her values written out in this way helped Aileen to realize that, while she was still fond of her husband, they had moved in very different directions. She realized that

she had been clinging to the security of what she had
known when, in her heart, she knew that it wasn't right for
her any more. She was then able to be proactive and to
make her own choice to end the marriage and to develop
her own, new life.

In the above example with Aileen, the decision-making didn't come by
simply ticking off the options against her written list of values. She used
it as part of a process of telling the truth about what mattered to her
and what she really wanted. Having a list of values helps you to listen to
yourself, as you consider something, and to remember what is really
important to you. You may still decide, after deep reflection, to choose
something that doesn't quite match up on paper and yet in your heart
you know is right for you. Just don't do it lightly.

Goals based around values

When goals are based around, or connected with, values they take on
more meaning and are easier to achieve. You are more likely to find
yourself pulled towards them rather than having to force yourself into
action. A common example is of setting goals around health and fitness.
If, for instance, your core values include family, nature and adventure then
you might set yourself a values-based goal of taking a week-long hike
together, in the summer vacation, along a mountain trail. As you spend
time discussing the trip and looking forward to it, you realize that it will
be far more enjoyable if you prepare for it by getting fitter and losing a
few pounds in weight over the next couple of months. Now you have a
values-based context for your health and fitness goals, which is far more
likely to keep you motivated than trying to lose weight and get fitter
simply because somebody says you 'ought to'.

Reflection point   ***Values-based goal***

What is one of your values which you would like to honour more in your life?

What 3-month goal would be an expression of that value?

Life purpose / personal contribution

An extension of working with values is to consider what your life purpose might be. Given your unique combination of values, talents and natural interests, what is the particular contribution that you are drawn to bring to the world around you? You can also think of this as your mission, your primary vision, or as the legacy that you want to leave. Some people think of this in terms of a life blueprint – a kind of soul contract or reason that they are here. Alternatively, you may think of it as something that evolves and becomes clearer as you live and develop – a sense of knowing how you can best play your part in life.

The upside of talking about and working with life purpose is that clarifying it and articulating it can give your life more perspective and meaning. The downside is that it can lead you to ignore what is really true for you and to look for something grandiose that you think will impress others and in some way justify your existence.

If you are true to yourself then you might find that your role involves playing a big part on the world stage and, then again, it might be something much quieter, personal and relatively unrecognized outside your close circle. For this reason, I sometimes prefer to talk about your natural expression or personal contribution, in the bigger scheme of things, as this can be less loaded. Use whichever terminology works best for you.

PERSONAL CASE STUDY ~ RECOGNISING YOUR CONTRIBUTION

In my early thirties, I spent a few years heavily involved in theatre. I studied dance and mime as well as taking a lot of acting courses. To subsidize all of this, I continued to work part time as head of Mathematics in a small, private college. I was a fairly good mime and clown and had some success with a clown-based theatre group. However, I aspired to be an actor, as I associated this with more meaning and status. In practice, I never did very well and seemed to be half-hearted in how I approached it. One day it dawned on me that this was not meant to happen. I asked myself what it was that I was really good at and what gave me satisfaction. The answer was a bit of a let down, at first, as I associated it with much less glamour and prestige. I realized that I was a really good educator in the original sense of educare, 'to draw forth from'. I derived my greatest satisfaction when empowering students to connect with themselves and, from that place, to achieve what they cared about. This was my calling. I saw that to be happy I had to give my own path status, whatever anybody else thought about it. Since then, in one form or another, these two elements of education and empowering have been part of everything I've done. Coaching is the best expression of them for me, so far.

As with values, the words you use to describe your life purpose are not what is really important. The words can be helpful but don't get hung up on them. As we said earlier, they are the fingers pointing at the moon, not the moon itself. Many people live very meaningful lives without ever having articulated a life purpose or a personal mission statement of any kind. It is the sense of doing what is right for you and being somehow connected to the bigger picture that matters. Some people also find that their purpose changes with different periods in their life. One client described to me how her primary purpose had shifted from being a mother, through being a healer, to her new stage – which she describes as learning 'to just be and respond to life' without logically thinking about or planning what comes out of it. Other people have reported something similar – a sense of tuning into their life unfolding in a natural order, rather than having a particular aim or description that they work from. There is no one right answer or formula, so experiment and find out what works best for you.

Approaches for clarifying your personal contribution

Here are a few tools for clarifying your personal contribution (or life purpose, if you prefer that term):

- Look at your values and reflect on what is your most fulfilling way of expressing them in the world.
- Reflect on your life and see if there are any recurrent themes concerning the times when you felt most inspired and fulfilled. How were you then expressing yourself and contributing to others?
- Think of the times when you felt most out of touch with yourself and your purpose. What was it that you were not doing or contributing? What was missing?

You can also use any of the various approaches to listening to yourself, given earlier in the chapter. For instance:

- Free writing or journaling about your contribution
- Writing a story of how you found your life purpose. One way to start this is with the words: 'Once upon a time there was a man/woman called (your name) who didn't know what they were meant to do in their life. So …'
- Using image work to connect with an inner mentor who reminds you of your purpose

A number of sample guided imageries are available for you to listen to on-line at the members' section of the web site www.self-factor.com.

Listening to yourself in the course of everyday life

So far we have mainly been considering approaches to listening to yourself where you take special time out from the busyness of the day. Now we will consider how you can connect with yourself during everyday activities. For this purpose we can consider attitudes, habits, systems and particular techniques.

Attitudes towards yourself

These were covered in some depth in chapter 4, on empowering yourself. In order to make it important enough to listen to yourself, you will want to cultivate an appreciation for yourself, your perceptions, your opinions and your wishes. This is developed and supported by how you talk to and about yourself and the language that you use. With the right attitudes, you will find it easier to stand up for yourself and your truth.

Habits and systems

If you develop ongoing, positive energy habits, and have supportive systems in place, it will be easier to be in a relaxed and resourceful state. Then you are more able to connect with what is going on with you and what you want in any given situation.

In contrast, if you are struggling by on adrenalin with unmet needs, chaotic structures and poor boundaries then it is going to be very difficult to know what you really think, feel and want at any time. The ever-present background static will prevent you from tuning into and listening clearly to yourself. Chapter 3, on sustaining yourself, looked at how to get more of your needs met and how to look after your energy. Chapter 4, on empowering yourself, had suggestions on how to manage agreements and boundaries.

Here are a few helpful ideas to consider:

- Schedule regular, free 'buffer' time in your diary to allow for unforeseen events. This also lets you take space from what you are involved in to stop, take stock and plan what to do next.
- Take regular lunchtimes and other breaks away from what you are doing so that your mind can re-group and integrate what you have been involved in.
- When you walk from one location to another, practice becoming more present, breathe more deeply and evenly and consciously notice your surroundings.
- Reduce your dependence on caffeine and adrenalin and, where possible, avoid sensory overload and negative people and situations. You don't have to wrap yourself in cotton wool or get over-precious about this. Just make healthier choices, where possible, so that you are in a more resourceful and responsive state more of the time.
- Review the section on positive energy habits, in chapter 3, and integrate some of these into your routine.

The cumulative effect of a number of small supportive background habits and structures keeps you more resourceful, and makes life a lot easier and enjoyable.

Techniques for listening to yourself during the day

Alongside setting things up so that you are generally in a more resourceful state, here are a few specific techniques for you to experiment with.

Holding an intention (or intentions) for the day

As well as setting intentions for what you want to achieve, you can set intentions for how you want to be and do things and how you would like to feel. For instance, you could set the intention to relax and to enjoy your work. It helps to have the intention written out somewhere where you will see it often and be reminded. At the beginning of the day, and of each section of work, read and re-affirm your intention, see how you are doing and notice what helps.

CASE STUDY ~ LARRY

Larry is a highly-skilled corporate coach working with senior executives and board members. By his own admission, Larry comes from a background of being very uptight and controlling. He knows that he does his best work, and is most effective, when he is relaxed, present, and fully responsive to the client in the moment. He finds this easiest when he connects with his own spiritual source and asks for help in serving the client as best he can. To support himself with this, he has an intentions list, of how he wants to be and operate, which he reads daily.

Stop times

In addition to scheduling in longer times, it is important to stop at different points throughout the day so that you can pause, reflect, organize your thinking and then move on. Even five minutes' pause can leave you more focused, resourceful and effective. Good times to call a stop break are when you are starting to feel stressed and when transitioning from one activity to another.

Use of powerful questions

At any time during the day, it can help to pause for a moment and ask yourself some key questions relating to what you are involved in, such as:

> What is important here?
> What do I think?
> What do I feel?
> What do I want?
> What is the best way to move forward here?

You can link these with checking in with what your body is telling you:

> What is my gut feeling about this?
> What does my heart tell me?

Mini versions of the taking time out approaches

Many of the earlier techniques we discussed, for clarifying situations and making decisions, can be adopted for use during a short stop break. One simple method that helps to ease your body, as well as free your mind, is to frame a question to hold and consider while going for a meditative five or ten minute stroll. Let the question rest in the background while you enjoy walking and becoming more present and aware of your surroundings. Even a trip to the bathroom or the photocopier can be a meditative time for reflection.

Dealing with others

We have already talked about the importance of setting up clear agreements and being able to maintain healthy boundaries.

It can also be helpful to give yourself time to reflect before responding to requests. You can sometimes put undue and unnecessary pressure on yourself by believing that you should always know what to do immediately. Thinking on your feet and 'just doing it' can be great skills when really needed. They can also be recipes for disaster. Without reflection and preparation, the solutions of today can often become the problems of tomorrow. 'Just doing it', as a dominant strategy, can lead to a lot of 'just undoing it' later! Simple as it may seem, learning to say 'maybe' or 'Let me think about that and then I'll get back to you' can be a godsend.

Reflection point **Giving yourself time before responding**

When, and with whom, do you need to give yourself more time before responding?

Key points

Listening to yourself lets you tap into your own vast store of experience, strength and wisdom. You can connect with yourself in many ways, using both right- and left-brain approaches, that complement each other.

Explore the different approaches to find out what works for you and don't get bogged down in them. Keep coming back to the basic questions:

- What is really true for you?
- What do you really want?
- What is the best way forward?

Truth-telling is essential since without it you have no solid foundation for moving forward. To get to what is really true for you can take persistence and an ongoing commitment.

As a basis for listening to yourself, you first want to be able to create space, become more present and quieten down. Methods for doing this include:

- Meditation
- Any activity which you enjoy and where you become more focused in present time

There are a variety of methods for clarifying situations and making decisions. Most include the use of words, whether thought, spoken or written. Alongside these methods are other, non-verbal techniques. Experiment with them but don't feel that you have to use them all. The different methods mentioned include:

Verbal approaches
- Reflection
- Power thinking
- Internal mentor and board of advisors
- Using an outside sounding board

Writing your way clear
- Listing key points
- Brainstorming
- Journaling
- Free writing
- Letters for your eyes only
- Metaphor
- Storytelling

Non-verbal approaches
- Accessing body wisdom
- Holding a question
- Maintaining an inquiry
- Guided imagery & image as metaphor
- Drawing and collage
- Movement, poetry and music

Feelings are a natural part of living. You need to be able to:
- access and express them appropriately
- manage them and put them to one side as needed

If your feelings are suppressed, or you are overwhelmed by them, it can help to work with a good counsellor or therapist.

The language that you use in connection with your feelings is important. Having a range of adjectives to describe your feelings makes for a richer inner landscape. Alongside this, you can choose language that helps keep negative feelings manageable and which emphasizes and enhances positive feelings.

Clarifying values is a way of acknowledging what you really care about and what brings you meaning and fulfilment. Having clarified your values, you can then find ways of honouring them more. Goals that are aligned with values are easier to achieve and bring more fulfilment.

Clarifying your life purpose, or personal contribution, is an extension of looking at your values. It can help you to see who you are, and what you do, as part of the bigger picture of things.

Listening to yourself during everyday life is an important life skill to be developed. It is much easier when you practise some of the earlier techniques, where you put special time aside for quietening down and for clarifying situations and making decisions.

You will also want to take care of your needs, have a positive attitude to yourself and your resources, and develop supportive habits and structures. Techniques for listening to yourself in activity include:

- Holding intentions for the day
- Stop times
- Using powerful questions
- Dealing with others

General tips

- Don't try to use all the techniques. Explore the ones that appeal most.
- Keep coming back to the basic questions:
  - What is really true for you?
  - What do you really want?
  - What is the best way forward?
- Be patient with yourself and keep a sense of humour
- Notice and celebrate all the positive shifts that you make

- Realize and accept that getting to know yourself is not a quick fix: it is an ongoing relationship

Setting intentions

If you need a reminder about holding intentions, take a look at chapter 2.

Possible intentions to hold include:

- Choose to listen to and connect with yourself more of the time
- Choose to tap into your own resources and to respect your own wisdom and opinions, rather than giving your power away to others
- Choose to develop and pay more attention to your intuition
- Choose to balance your intuition with clear thinking and discernment
- Choose to become more present in your life and to live less in the past and in the future
- Choose to take responsibility for feeling, expressing and managing your emotions
- Choose to live life according to your values
- Choose to align with your life purpose

Taking action

Remember, from chapter 2, that actions which come out of raising your awareness and holding an intention to change will be the most powerful. To start with, choose things that are a stretch but not too threatening. Focus on no more than three at any one time.

The following actions are some ideas to get you started:

- Spend at least 20 minutes each day in quietening down your mind, whether you use meditation or some other activity to help you. Schedule time for this in your diary.

- Schedule in regular time for reflection and planning. Treat these times as appointments with yourself, to be kept to as rigorously as if they were appointments with someone else.
- Each week, for the next four weeks, choose one new technique from this chapter to practice. At the end of the four weeks, choose one of these techniques to practice regularly for the following month.
- For one week, commit to monitoring and choosing language that keeps negative feelings in perspective and emphasizes positive feelings.
- Spend one hour this week clarifying your values. List them where you will see them regularly. Keep amending and updating them until you feel that they really reflect the essence of what you are about.
- Set one goal this month that is an expression of one of your values.
- Spend an hour reflecting on your life and the times when you felt most alive and fulfilled. See if there are any recurring themes, and ask yourself what your life purpose might be, in the greater scheme of things.
- Make at least one, specific change this week so that you are more aligned with your purpose.
- From chapter 3, choose five positive energy habits to do daily for the next month.
- Practise giving yourself some reflection time before agreeing to any requests.

6 ~ Friendship with Your Self

In a sense, the whole of this book has been about how to become your own best friend. That is the backdrop to everything we have looked at together and is more to do with basic attitudes than particular techniques, although these can be helpful. At each point you have been encouraged both to accept yourself as you are and to make the most of yourself and your opportunities. At its richest, friendship is a gift that you give yourself – the gift of unconditional support.

As a good friend you will sustain, empower and listen to yourself. You will find that some of this chapter re-states and reinforces ideas that have gone before. Given that many of us have learned to distrust and undermine ourselves over a lifetime, you will find that you benefit from coming back to the new and more positive perspectives time and time again.

The relationship with yourself is the only one that is 24/7 and is guaranteed to be there for the rest of your life. Hence I call it the primary relationship. As well as being the basis for good relationships with other people, how you relate to and think about yourself determines who you will allow yourself to be, what you will allow yourself to do and what you will allow yourself to achieve.

Being a good friend to yourself is not about cheesy affirmations or self-indulgence. It is about really caring and wanting the best for yourself and being willing to give yourself whatever It takes to live a personally meaningful and fulfilled life. Sometimes that will mean giving yourself the equivalent of a warm hug and sometimes it will be more like a well-timed kick in the butt.

FINDHORN
Press

Tel 01309 690582 / Freephone 0800 389 9395
Fax 01309 690036
e-mail info@findhornpress.com
www.findhornpress.com

Thank you for choosing this book. We appreciate your interest and support.
If you would like to receive our full catalogue of books card sets and cds,
please fill in this card and mail it to us.

☐ Please send Findhorn Press latest catalogue
☐ Please send information about the Findhorn Foundation in Scotland

In which book did you find this card?

Where did you buy this book?

Please write
your name and
address here
(please PRINT)

What is your email address?

Reflection point   **How good a friend are you to yourself?**

How good a friend are you to yourself?

In what ways could you be a better friend to yourself?

What are you willing to start doing differently?

We'll take a look at the different types of friendship you can develop with other people and then see how you can incorporate aspects of these into being a good friend to yourself.

Different types of friendship

People are drawn to be friends for different reasons. Part of being human is our need for companionship and support – to spend time with people that we know and like, who know and like us in return, and who are our allies in different endeavours. In recent decades, changes in society and how we live have affected how we approach, and what we expect from, friendship.

Traditional friendships

In the past, friendships were mostly based on shared backgrounds and shared interests.

Shared backgrounds

When people tended to stay in one place and follow a fairly predictable track in life, a lot of friendships arose from shared backgrounds – people with the same kind of upbringing and cultural roots as yourself. These friendships came with extended family connections where everyone knew everyone else and even shared similar jobs, hobbies and political views. Moving outside your own local area, let alone to a different part of the country, was a big deal. While these shared backgrounds still play a big part in some people's lives, they are less fixed than they used to be. It is now much more common, through education and work, for people to cross social, economic and even national boundaries. Extended families play a smaller part in a lot of people's lives and, in many cases, friendships come to take their place. Whether or not these changes are a good thing is open to debate; there are both costs and benefits in any transition. Whether we like it or not, though, we are all affected by the degree of change going on around us and need to respond to it as well as we can, including how we cultivate and maintain friendships.

Shared interests

Social changes mean that friendships are now more often associated with shared personal and work interests. You might watch movies with one friend and share your love of sport with another. Friendships may be built around children, work or whatever, and it is not uncommon for friendships to drop away and for you to acquire new friends as your interests and focus change. In fact, with changes of job, partnership and location becoming far more frequent in people's lives, many of us find that we don't have the continuum in friendship that was more common in previous days. Hence friendships that can embrace you as you continue to change and evolve are particularly valuable. There are certain friends with whom the connection is deep and lasting, even when you don't see each other for a while and when interests, focus and lifestyle change.

Deeper friendships

There are many components of deep friendship that, while they include companionship, go beyond shared interests and spending time together. There is a sense of being known, accepted and appreciated beyond the surface layers of how you appear in the world. There are those people who believe in you and are there for you during both the ups and downs of life. Without acceptance, friendship is very limited. Yet, in deep friendship, acceptance doesn't always means agreeing with each other or pretending that things are okay when they are not. A good friendship includes being open and truthful with each other. When you want the best for someone, occasionally you will tell them what you think they need to hear. You will also let them know if you are unhappy about something so that you can clear the air and stay connected, without unspoken resentment coming between you.

One thing that perhaps best distinguishes deep and lasting friendship is that your friend is someone who is there for you whatever – a friend who encourages you and celebrates your success when you are up and is equally ready to hold your hand and accept you when you are down. Often, friends are either good weather friends or bad weather friends.

Good weather friends

Some friends are fair weather friends only, ready to abandon or condemn you when you fail or don't live up to expectations. Shakespeare comments on this in the play within the play in *Hamlet* Act 3, Scene 2, where these lines are spoken by the player king:

> '... .... 'tis not strange,
> That even our loves should with our fortunes change:
> For 'tis a question left us yet to prove,
> Whether love lead fortune, or else fortune love.
> The great man down, you mark, his favourite flies;
> The poor advanc'd makes friends of enemies.
> And hitherto doth love on fortune tend:
> For who not needs shall never lack a friend;
> And who in want a hollow friend doth try,
> Directly seasons him his enemy.'

In our hearts, we all know that the kinds of friendship and appreciation that only come with outward success are limited and hollow. Chasing them can lead you to sell out on yourself and to do things for the sake of how they look to others, rather than because they align with your own values. Being successful can mean different things to different people; that is not the problem. However it looks, when success comes from authentically being and expressing yourself, it is a great and empowering experience. The problem arises when you put superficial success before your integrity, meaning and fulfilment.

Bad weather friends

Perhaps not so obvious is the opposite scenario. Some people are not only willing to be with you through the bad times but are actually more at ease with you when sharing about what has gone wrong, who is to blame and how generally awful life is. They feel uncomfortable with you when you are doing well. They subtly undermine you or cause you to doubt or sabotage yourself with apparently well-meant words of caution. The implication is that the good guys are the ones who are having a hard time. Anyone who is happy and successful must be well out of integrity, if not actually having done a deal with the devil — they will get their comeuppance sooner or later, in this life or the next!

You have only to read a newspaper or watch the news to know that our society as a whole is tuned into negativity and victim-hood. Behind the ever-ready words of sympathy, these kinds of friends can covertly hold you back from your potential success and happiness. This does not mean that they consciously wish you harm, or that they are bad people; their own belief and survival systems are heavily invested in keeping the status quo. One of the challenges in breaking away from this way of relating is that sharing wounds can become addictive and feel synonymous with intimacy.

Reflection
point   **Good or bad weather friends?**

Are you more at ease when sharing and celebrating success or when commiserating with difficulties?

Which, if either, are your friendships mostly based on?

Are there any friendships from which you need to move on?

When it comes to outward success, I have known and worked with a great variety of people. My experience is that neither rich nor poor have a monopoly on either happiness or suffering. Provided that your main needs are met, meaning and fulfilment are connected with how you live and whether or not you do the things that you really care about, however they look to the outside world. Living a meaningful life may or may not, then, go with money and material success.

All weather friends

What is rarer, and hence particularly valuable, is a friend who is there for you through both the highs and the lows: someone who supports you through the bad times while continuing to want the best for you; someone who can see you and accept you at your lowest, warts and all, and who still believes in you, encourages you and is there ready to celebrate the good times with you. This is part of what can come out of the most successful marriages, when partners have been through both the ups and downs together, and become each other's closest friend. As it becomes more and more common for relationships to change, one of the most positive outcomes following a separation is for lovers to transition into friends. This takes time and doesn't always work out, but if you can retain the friendship aspect then you still have a valuable relationship, albeit in a different form.

Friends growing together

By this I don't mean getting bigger in bulk, even though I notice that increased maturity and consciousness have a tendency to be accompanied by a corresponding expansion in waistband. The mathematician in me wonders if there is a formula along the lines of $e = mc^2$, where e stands for expansion, m for maturity and c for the consciousness factor. If anyone develops this for a thesis, don't forget to credit me with the original idea ... .

Anyway, by growing together, I mean friendships that are based on, or include, ways of learning and evolving together.

From co-dependent to inter-developmental

Stephen R. Covey, author of *The Seven Habits of Highly Effective People* (Simon & Schuster, 2004), talks about a continuum of maturity from dependence through independence to interdependence. Thomas Leonard, one of the leading pioneers of coaching and the founder of Coach U, adapted this model to a five step continuum for relationships:

> Inter-developmental
> Interdependent
> Independent
> Dependent
> Co-dependent

As I use the terms, co-dependency relates to a victim mentality and making each other responsible for your feelings and limitations. Dependency has elements of this and, though not as dysfunctional, each partner still depends on the other to an extent that limits their ability to express themselves and to achieve things. In developing independence you become pro-active and emphasize that you are responsible for your experiences, your life and your choices. As you become stronger in this, and continue to grow in awareness, you see a bigger picture and realize that life as a whole is an interdependent, organic system. You learn to co-operate with other independent people and to form healthy, interdependent relationships. Then the power of synergy allows you to produce greater and more fulfilling results than you can each achieve alone. Inter-developmental relationships are interdependent relation-ships which further support each other in continuing to grow and develop.

This is a great model for inspiring and informing change and, as with all ideals, it can have its downside if you try and force it to happen or use it to judge yourself and give yourself a hard time. Trying to live out an image of super responsible, aware and inter-developmental good guy can be very tiring. Sometimes you just need to hang out and, where your personal shortcomings are really not such a big deal, let yourself be. Keep a sense of humour about it and maybe even claim your foibles as part of your personal style.

The four elements of the SELF model that we have been exploring are different aspects of developing a strong sense of self so that you are able to be independent and pro-active. More than that, they are a way of maintaining that strong sense of self, including embracing your own humanness, as you engage in fulfilling, interdependent and inter-developmental relationships.

From fixing to supporting

When you work together inter-developmentally, supporting each other is about empowering rather than fixing. It is acknowledging the power of synergy to allow both individuals and teams to become stronger and more effective. This is the context in which coaching works. The assumption is that you have the resources and answers you need and that the coach supports you in drawing on your resources and generating and acting on your own answers. It is becoming more and more common for organizations, in addition to using external coaches, to invest in developing a coaching culture where managers and teams coach each other. In personal relationships, too, rather than assuming that the other needs fixing, you can take the time to listen and to give your attention as they explore their own way forward.

Reflection point *Your current relationships*

Take a moment to reflect on your personal and work relationships.

Write down two main work relationships and two main personal relationships.

For each relationship, where are they on the continuum from co-dependent to inter-developmental?

What would be involved in having these relationship grow?

What is a first step that you can take this coming week?

Being a friend to yourself

Having explored what the possibilities are in friendships with others, we now look at how you can integrate them into your friendship with yourself. This will provide you with a foundation of appreciation and encouragement, which is there whoever you are with and whatever you are doing. This is not to replace your external relationships but rather to give you a better chance of enjoying them.

Enjoying your own company

We noted that companionship is a part of most friendships and so it is important that you enjoy your own company. Aloneness is not the same as loneliness and for most people there is a healthy balance between time alone and time spent with others. If you are not comfortable being alone, you can end up hanging out with people, and doing things, that you don't even like, if the truth is told. In contrast, if you enjoy your own company then this allows you to seek the company of others because you enjoy being with them, rather than because you are trying to get away from yourself. Even if you are comfortable with being alone, you may find that you don't make enough time for it.

CASE STUDY ~ NANCY

Nancy worked in the city. She was caught up in a social life that was no longer nourishing her and which frequently left her feeling tired and empty, as well as draining her finances. She found herself unable to say 'no' to any invitation and hardly ever spent a quiet evening at home alone. As we discussed what was happening, Nancy realized how little she now enjoyed this frenetic pace and that it was important that she start to make changes. Together we explored how she might enjoy time with herself, including some quiet time without TV. She got excited at the possibilities and really wanted to do it. Nancy decided, as an initial experiment, to schedule in two nights per week just for herself. We then figured out strategies for how to deal with invitations and pressures from other people. Part of this was to consider the evenings in as appointments with herself, to be treated with the same respect as appointments with other people. To help her with this, she then practised role playing how to say 'no' gracefully. Nancy now really enjoys regular time alone and also finds that she is more discerning of how she spends time with others. When she does go out she now enjoys it much more.

Reflection point   **Spending time alone**

How are you with spending time alone and enjoying your own company?

Are you able to say 'no', to things and people, so that you have your time alone?

How much time alone is good for you and how much time do you make for it?

What changes, if any, do you need to make?

Appreciation

Another aspect of friendship is feeling appreciated, and it is important that you learn to appreciate yourself fully. It is worth remembering the three main definitions of 'to appreciate':

- To value highly and be grateful for
- To be aware of and understand
- To develop in value

All three aspects are part of a deep and lasting friendship with yourself, and we have looked at them in different sections of the book. In chapter 4, about empowering yourself, we looked at the impact of attitudes and belief cycles and how important it is to have a deep respect for yourself and your potential. This comes from a combination of how you think, the language you use, the things you do, and the way that you emphasize different experiences. In chapter 5, about listening to yourself, we focused on getting to know and understand yourself and being able to tap into different aspects of yourself. The book as a whole is about developing yourself and links in with how we talked about inter-developmental relationships with other people.

Being there, through the ups and downs

Having an all-weather friendship with yourself is absolutely essential as you are the only one who is with you all of the time, 24/7, for life – and maybe even longer, depending on your belief system. If you are not ready to accept yourself, whatever is going on for you, you will try to escape with drink, drugs, co-dependent relationships, being a workaholic, or some other form of addiction.

You can get stuck in being just a good weather friend to yourself, only feeling okay when things are going well for you. Equally, you can get stuck in being a bad weather friend. You can make a virtue out of being a victim and try to convince yourself that it is better to stay on the ground than risk getting up and falling down again. The reality is that, for most of us, life is a roller coaster. We need to find a place of stability, within us, that allows us to be at peace with both the highs and the lows. There is a story of an ancient king who went to his wise advisors and asked how he could be less at the mercy of changing events. After reflection, they had a ring made for him, on the inside of which was engraved the words 'This too shall pass'.

Reflection point   **Through the ups and downs**

Are you there for yourself whatever, or do you abandon yourself sometimes?

How can you support yourself more through both the ups and the downs?

Balancing acceptance and expectation

There is a balance between accepting yourself and your situation, as things are now, and encouraging yourself to dream, to engage your intention and to make new and better things happen. If you simply settle for the status quo, you are in danger of living a half life and denying what you do want and what really matters to you. You become afraid to try something new in case it doesn't work out or things get worse.

On the other hand, if you identify your self-worth only with external achievement, you can become addicted to a life of strain and struggle, where you never give yourself a chance to rest or to appreciate what you have already got and done. You may acquire the common behavioural 'dis-ease' that I call 'next-syndrome'. This is when you accomplish a goal that was important to you and, without any rest or celebration, you simply say 'next!' Living life in this way can look good to the outside world but if you become addicted to struggle, and measure yourself only by achievement, then this becomes another kind of status quo and is equally unfulfilling. For some people, doing less can be as scary and challenging as doing more is for others.

Both extremes tend to equate self-worth with what you have got and done. One is more motivated by the fear of losing what you've got while the other is more motivated by the fear of not having enough. The way forward is to combine unconditional self-acceptance with positive expectation and a spirit of adventure. It is to be a friend to yourself and to know that you are okay whatever is going on, good or bad, and whatever you do or do not achieve. Then, alongside this, to value yourself enough to give yourself the best chance of having and doing what matters to you, just because it does. There is an inner freedom that comes with knowing that whatever you do cannot make you okay – because you are already okay to start with.

Being your own great boss

In a work context we can talk about the characteristics and attitude of an ideal boss or leader. This is someone who really appreciates who you are and what you do and, from that positive foundation, empowers you to take on new projects and to try out new possibilities – someone who makes it safe to take considered risks and who will not blame you if things don't work out. Whether you are self-employed or an employee there is always a sense in which you work for yourself and contract out your services to other people. If you don't like your work conditions, you can always choose to end or not renew the contract and to work with somebody else. Start now to be a great boss to yourself.

Reflection point   **Being a good boss to yourself**

What kind of 'boss' are you to yourself?

How much do you drive yourself and how much do you take care of your own welfare?

What would it be like to initiate a 'no blame' culture in your life and work?

Moving outside your comfort zone

Any significant change of thinking or behaviour will require you to move outside your comfort zone. (We looked at this in chapter 2, about changing for a change.) By definition, it nearly always involves some form of short term discomfort and is often accompanied by more or less fear. At these times, you will benefit from the encouragement and reassurance of a good friend – starting with yourself. You want to acknowledge yourself for having the courage to try something new and also to remind yourself that it is okay and natural to feel uneasy at times. The pace at which you initiate and maintain change needs to be both motivating and self-friendly. It has to suit your particular needs and style.

Go too slowly and you lose motivation: push too quickly and you increase fear and resistance and the likelihood of giving up. In reality, there is no one-size-fits-all and this can prove to be the limitation of many trainings and workshops. Part of the power of individual coaching, whether alone or as a follow-up to training, is that the individual gets to set the agenda and to adapt the different models to work for them. This is why you have been encouraged throughout this book to think for yourself, to choose to take on what is right for you now and to leave the rest or else come back to it later. So, tell the truth about how much you are ready to take on and what is the right pace for you at any particular time.

Reflection point   **What pace is right for you?**

When you move outside your comfort zone, what do you need from yourself?

What is the right pace to keep you motivated without going into overwhelm?

Seeing the bigger picture

It is also important that you are a friend to yourself in the bigger picture – that of taking your place in the world.

So who do you think you are?

Many years ago, in the early days of my own personal growth journey, I tried out a great variety of approaches and techniques. Some of them were mainstream and some were wild and wacky. Some were soon to be forgotten and some left a permanent, positive impact. One of the most interesting had a very simple structure – the whole time you stayed focused on the single question, 'Who am I?' Some of the time you would pair up with a partner and take turns to ask each other the question, 'Tell me who you are.' When you were the one being asked the question, you paused, noticed what came up in response to the question, and then communicated your experience to your partner. They were simply present to hear you without comment. Other times you just reflected on the question alone. Apart from the partner exercise, there was no other talking throughout the workshop. I did one three-day event like this and later a ten-day version. Initially, I would say all the usual things, such as that I was a teacher, that I was in a relationship with so-and-so, and all the other ways that I showed up in the world. Then, as the thoughts quietened down, emotions would surface and I experienced many other parts and aspects of myself. Then there came a deeper level again, quieter and fuller – not an intellectual thought but rather a deeper and enduring sense of being and knowing, best expressed simply as 'I am me'. Staying with this deeper sense of 'me-ness' there was then an additional awareness of being linked with everything else and of being one with the whole.

Similar experiences occur in meditation retreats or other times away from the hustle and bustle of everyday living. My guess is that many, if not most, people experience something like this at different times in their life. It is a sense of being both unique and at one with everyone and everything else.

A similar, outer journey, paralleling this inner one, occurs in the continuum model of relationships described earlier. Alongside behavioural changes there are paradigm changes of consciousness. At the level of dependence, there is an emphasis on you taking care of and being responsible for me. As independence is strengthened, there is more of an emphasis on the I who is separate and responsible. As inter-dependence is developed, the sense of I is balanced by a sense of what we can do together and our shared responsibility and possibilities. At first this may primarily be linked to the family or the group. It then continues to expand, beyond even a tribal or national consciousness, until it becomes global and planetary.

This expanded sense of consciousness changes who and what you identify with and what you consider to be your own self-interest. It is not surprising that virtually every major religion has its own version of the Christian dictum, 'Do unto others as you would have done unto yourself.' This is, perhaps, even more applicable today than at any time. In the UK, a recent survey conducted by Channel 4 showed that this was the paradigm that people, of all ages and places in society, thought most important to live by.

There has been an exponential growth in consciousness and bigger-picture thinking in recent years. This has come about partly as a result of global communication through television and the internet. And partly, perhaps, as a survival response to the state of the planet and the dire conditions of third world countries, which has implications for everyone. There is a far greater sense of belonging to one global family then ever before and a growing realization that we cannot isolate our own future from the future of other nations and people.

So why bring all of this into a discussion on friendship with yourself? Because, as your sense of who you are and what you identify with expands, treating yourself well goes hand in hand with treating other people well. Then making a contribution is not about duty or burden but about being a friend to yourself, from the perspective of the bigger picture. That is why half of the royalties from this book are going to help third world charities. It's a way of treating myself well.

I believe that, as a species and as a planet, our only hope is to develop a more global consciousness and that this is now too important to be thought of as anything but a mainstream concern. Alternative organizations who have in the past broadly labelled all of industry as 'the enemy' must now put aside prejudices and work with them to find solutions. Corporations, that have dragged their heels in the past, must realize that more and more of their constituents want to make a more positive contribution to a shared world. Voluntary environmental policies are slowly on the increase and both workers and management want to be associated with more ethical practices. We must all become inter-developmental.

Let's end this section on inter-relatedness with a poem from the Vietnamese Buddhist teacher, Thich Nhat Hanh:

Interrelationship

You are me, and I am you.
Isn't it obvious that we "inter-are"?
You cultivate the flower in yourself,
so that I will be beautiful.
I transform the garbage in myself,
so that you will not have to suffer.

I support you;
you support me.
I am in this world to offer you peace;
you are in this world to bring me joy.'

Reprinted from *Call Me By My True Names: The Collected Poems of Thich Nhat Hanh* (1999) by Thich Nhat Hanh with permission of Parallax Press, Berkeley, California, www.parallax.org

Committing 24/7 for life

Any deep relationship will go through many stages as you grow and change with time and experience. So it is with the relationship with yourself. It takes time and commitment and can develop over a lifetime. I have a better and more supportive relationship with myself now than at any point in my life. And I still have times when I am off form, grumpy or moody and generally out of synch with myself. I don't take these 'bad me' days so seriously anymore and, even when I feel emotionally challenged, at a deeper level I still know and feel that I am okay. The sense of being there for myself is relatively constant.

Part of what helped bring this about was recovering from a separation a number of years ago. It had been a very intense relationship and the break up was equally intense. Somehow the experience helped me to realize, and to take on board fully, that the relationship with myself was the only one that I could be sure was going to last for life. More than that, there was no option for divorce. Like it or not, it was always 24/7. Wherever I was, whatever I did and whatever I said, I would always be the one there doing and saying. The one person that I could never get away from was myself. This is true for you, too, whether you are being a lover, a parent, a manager, a colleague or any one of the myriad roles you undertake. The one person who is always involved is you. So why not decide to be the best you that you can and to be a good friend to yourself?

My own experience led me to a decision: I chose to make the primary relationship with myself the best I could and to commit to being there for me, whatever. As a symbol of that commitment I bought myself a ring to remind me. Inside is an inscription in Gaelic – *tha gaol agam ort* which roughly translates as 'my love is upon thee'. And that is what my journey and this book are really about – learning to love yourself as you engage with and bring your unique contribution to the world. It is only when you love yourself that you can fully love another. Otherwise there is always an element of using them to escape from yourself.

Being in balance and moving forward

There are many different aspects to living in balance. We have looked at some of these in previous chapters and we shall consider more in the next chapter, on vision, intention and goals. In this chapter, we have talked about the balance between acceptance and expectation and lastly about the balance between you as an individual and you as part of a greater whole. It is tempting to think that you can approach all of this on a purely logical basis, and apportion time and resources accurately and consistently. In reality, different areas are not so black and white and they interweave. Balance tends to occur over an extended period of time rather than being fixed and consistent. It is like riding a bicycle where balance is maintained by a series of oscillations around the midpoint.

In a similar way, progress and growth often occurs in spurts and there are fallow periods as well as more productive ones. The 'two steps forward and one step back' experience is part of it. This applies as much to building a better relationship with yourself as it does to achieving your goals. I mention this here so that, when the natural downturns occur, you can remember to keep a positive perspective rather than going into doom and gloom and abandoning yourself.

Key points

Friendship with yourself is the overview that guides and informs the rest of the book. The chapters on sustaining, empowering and listening give practical ideas on how to be a good friend to yourself. Conversely, the attitude of friendship with yourself will allow you to get the most out of the other sections.

The primary relationship, with yourself, is the only one that is guaranteed for life and the only one that is 24/7. Wherever you are, whatever you do and whatever you say, you are the one who is there doing and saying. You are the one friend who can always be present for you.

Friendship with yourself is not against or instead of external friendship. It is the foundation for it.

There are different types of external friendship including:

- Friendship based on shared background
- Friendship based on shared interests
- Deeper, evolving friendship – adapting as you change and grow

Aspects of deeper friendships include:

- All weather friendship
  - embracing both the highs and the lows
- Inter-developmental
  - interdependent relationships supporting mutual growth
- Supporting each other rather than fixing

The continuum model of relationships is a progression of awareness and behaviour, from co-dependent to inter-developmental.

Inter-developmental

Interdependent

Independent

Dependent

Co-dependent

In practice, progress is not as clear cut and linear as the ideal would suggest. There will be times and areas of your life where you revert to less aware and healthy behaviour. Hence it is important to continue to be a good friend to yourself, to accept your humanness and sometimes to cut yourself some slack. Then, from this place of self-acceptance, you can come back to doing the best that you can because you care about and value yourself – not because you 'should'.

Aspects of being a good friend to yourself include:

- Enjoying your own company
- Appreciating yourself
  - o valuing, understanding and developing
- Supporting yourself through both the highs and the lows
- Balancing acceptance and expectation
- Being a great boss to yourself
- Supporting yourself as you move outside your comfort zone
- Expanding your sense of self to include being:
  - o both unique and part of the whole
- Commitment to yourself
- Living in balance

General tips

- Start from wherever you are and don't give yourself a hard time
- When you find yourself being unfriendly or critical to yourself:
  ○ Keep a sense of humour and don't take it too seriously
  ○ Don't criticize yourself for being critical
  ○ Breathe, and start again
- Remember that the best reason to grow and change is because you care enough about yourself to do so
- Where possible, spend time with, and get the support of, similar-minded people who also want to grow and be positive

Setting intentions

If you need a reminder about holding intentions then take a look at chapter 2.

Possible intentions to hold are:

- Choose to become a better friend to yourself
- Choose to motivate yourself through encouragement rather than criticism
- Choose to cultivate inter-developmental friendships with others
- Choose to spend some quality time alone each week
- Choose to appreciate yourself
- Choose to be an all-weather friend to yourself
- Choose to be a great boss to yourself
- Choose to extend your comfort zone
- Choose to commit to yourself
- Choose to live more in balance

Since the earlier chapters all contribute to the friendship with yourself, you can also use any of the intentions and actions from those chapters.

Taking action

Remember, from chapter 2, that actions which come out of raising your awareness and holding an intention to change will be the most powerful. To start with, choose things that are a stretch but not too threatening. Focus on no more than three at any one time.

The following actions are some ideas to get you started:

- Spend at least 20 minutes each day quietening down your mind and connecting with yourself. Schedule time for this in your diary.
- Each week, schedule some fun time on your own, where you can enjoy your own company – this could be walking, reading, listening to music or whatever.
- Write an appreciations list of yourself, your qualities and your achievements. Do this over a week.
- For one week, only motivate yourself through encouragement. If you find yourself being critical, don't give yourself a hard time. Just start again with encouragement.
- Every day for a week, do at least one thing that takes you outside your comfort zone. Pace yourself so that you do things that stretch you but are manageable and don't put you in physical or economic danger.
- Look at the balance in your life and choose one area that has been neglected. For the next two weeks, focus on improving that area.

7 ~ Vision, Intention and Goals

This book is primarily about developing and maintaining a strong relationship with and sense of self, and we could have a whole other book around goal setting and strategizing. Here we will take just a brief look at how to work with vision, intention and goals in such a way that you continue to develop and maintain a good connection with yourself.

Goal-setting in context

Used well, goal-setting can be one of the basic tools in creating a life of meaning and fulfilment. Goals that are aligned with your values and purpose, and are an expression of who you are and what you really care about, motivate you into action. Achieving this kind of positive goal gives you a healthy feeling of accomplishment, confidence and satisfaction.

On the other hand, goals are commonly chosen in accordance with someone else's agenda, because you think that you should do them or because you are using them, in some way, to prove that you are okay. This kind of goal tends to become a burden, involve a lot of struggle and procrastination and brings little genuine satisfaction. For some people, achieving becomes a superficial measure of their self-worth, regardless of whether what they achieve has any real meaning for them or for anybody else.

So, setting life and business goals that align with your greater purpose, values and vision is the ideal for which we aim. In practice, life is never quite that clear cut and there is likely to be a certain amount of static that gets in the way of tuning into yourself and living from this ideal. You may first need to deal with some urgent problems in front of you and to handle some unmet needs and other energy drains. You may also need to develop new attitudes and skills so that you are more empowered to move forward and to stand up for what you really care about. Hence the chapters on sustaining and empowering yourself come early in the book.

When doing this preparatory work, if you can keep in mind that it is a foundation for living your ideal, it will have more meaning and you will find it easier to tackle. It is like having a vision for a beautiful garden, while acknowledging that what you are starting with is a bit overgrown and rocky and that you lack some of the knowledge and skills that you will need. Doing the clearing and studying will be much easier if you can stay in touch with your vision for the garden. As the ground is cleared, and you learn more, you will be able to see more clearly what is possible. Then you can update and expand on your vision and may need to do further clearing and learning. It is a continuing cycle.

It may also be the case that, at some times and in some areas of your life, you are happy to go with the flow and watch things unfold rather than consciously planning how you want things to be. This is perfectly valid provided that you take responsibility for accepting how things turn out this way. If you are not happy with how things are, you will want to start making some choices and taking some action to create change.

Clarifying desired outcomes

Conscious change happens as a result of looking at a particular area of your life or business and making choices about how you want things to be. Depending on your style, and how things are going, you will find it helpful to go into more or less detail. It is a bit like having a camera with a zoom lens. First you choose what to point the camera at and then, depending on your needs, you can zoom in to get more detail or else zoom out to get more perspective.

From primary vision to goals and action steps

Your primary vision is a generalized, big-picture perspective of how you want to be living your life, how you want to be relating to other people and what you want to be doing. For your life to have meaning, and for you to be fulfilled, you will want your primary vision to align with your values and your life purpose (which we looked at in chapter 5, about listening to yourself).

Starting from this big picture, of what you want your life to be about, you can then zoom in to progressively more detail, as you clarify your longer term and shorter term visions for different areas of your life. For a vision to become actualized, you need to engage your intention and take pro-active responsibility for making it happen. You move from saying 'I would like this' to 'I want this' and then, even more powerfully, to 'I will have this' or 'I will do this'.

In some cases, it may be that what works best for you is simply to hold your vision and intentions clearly, to do what you do and to notice and respond to what happens. This is often easiest to do, and most likely to succeed, in areas where you already have some experience of setting and achieving goals. In most cases, however, the most effective way to move forward and reach your vision will be to set additional, specific goals and to use commitment and accountability to help you.

Stages involved in achieving an outcome

- Establish a Focus
  - Choose which area(s) of your life or business to focus on
- Explore the Current Reality
  - Take time to appreciate what is already happening
- Develop a Vision
  - Imagine, as vividly as possible, how you want things to be
- Engage Your Intention

- ○ Engage your intention so that 'I would like' becomes 'I want' or even more powerfully 'I will have' or 'I will do'
- Set Goals
  - ○ SMART goals are: Specific, Measurable, Achievable, Realistic and Time-oriented
- Plan Action Steps
  - ○ Develop a particular strategy with milestones along the way
- Take Action
  - ○ Carry out your plan(s) and action steps
- Generate and Respond to Feedback
  - ○ Monitor what happens and re-assess your vision, goals and strategy

ANSWERS for success

It can be helpful to realize that you are already naturally successful at achieving some goals and that you are doing it all the time. When it comes to achieving a new, desired outcome, you can think about how you already get something to happen in everyday life. For instance, you can reflect on how you manage to reach a specific destination or to get a cup of tea. Suppose I decide that I would like a cup of tea. I know clearly what I mean by having a cup of tea. I say 'I want a cup of tea' (acknowledging the gap between what is and what I want) while *knowing* that I can have one. Then, if I want it *enough,* either I make one myself or I get somebody else to make it for me. If there are obstacles, such as no tea bags in the cupboard, then I go to the shop, borrow from a neighbour or do something else. I keep adapting to circumstances, and trying new options, until I reach my goal and get the tea. Or else, if I don't care enough about the goal, then I will let it go.

There are seven aspects that may be involved in reaching a goal or vision. It can be useful to consider them before starting out on a new venture. Ask yourself some questions about each of the seven areas and see how the answers add up. Use the acronym, ANSWERS, to help you.

The ANSWERS model

Aim – Clarifying the vision.

That is, knowing what you want clearly enough to say whether or not it happens.

Now – Acknowledging current reality & creating the gap.

This involves telling the truth about 'what is' and where you are starting from. Also being willing to deal with it so that you move forward from a solid foundation.

Stance – Strengthening your sense of knowing that the vision is possible for you.

This could involve reflecting on past successes, relating your goal to what others have done, chunking down to smaller steps that you know you can achieve, affirmations, getting additional support, and more.

Wanting – Strengthening your wanting of the result so that emotional, creative energy is behind the vision. Do you really want it? What are the consequences of getting it, or not? How would you need to amend your vision to make it more attractive?

Energy – Making enough energy available. A great car going to a great destination still needs fuel. Do you have the necessary energy available to enable you to stay motivated and in action? If not, what else in your life needs to change?

Resources – Having the necessary resources. You need appropriate experience, skills, time, people and physical resources to enable you to reach your outcomes. If they are not in place, a first step may be to work on getting them.

Strategy – Clarifying how you will do it. What are the actions-steps? Are the strategies worth it? Are they appropriate for the available energy and resources?

All aspects need to mesh together. If you don't believe it is possible then it would be foolish to let yourself want it; that would be courting failure, so why take action? If the actions you envisage are not worth the cost, you will not really engage or else you will self-sabotage. If you don't really want it and are living somebody else's script then you will be *trying* to want it which is hard work! If you are already stressed out then the last thing you need is a new project. Although all the areas interconnect, it can still be very helpful to ask yourself which one may be missing or need attention first.

Lastly, but very importantly, you may be motivating yourself by implying that you will only be okay once you have achieved your goal. This can produce results but at a great cost since, in reality, you are always in process. If you have finally arrived at a state where nothing else is possible, then they call that state death! So it is much better to accept yourself now and, from that place of acceptance and okayness, to choose to express yourself in your projects.

The ANSWERS model is also useful to consider when you find that your goal is not really happening. Look through the seven parts and ask yourself which one may be blocking you. You will also need to address any self-sabotage or procrastination.

Self-sabotage and procrastination

Do you sometimes seem to be your own worst enemy? And do you sometimes find yourself engaging in counter-productive activities or else failing to follow through on your plans and intentions, even though nothing really seems to be in your way? If you do, then you are part of a very big club. Blaming yourself is unlikely to help and you need to look a little deeper for a solution.

If you assume that there is an enemy or saboteur within, whose primary intention is to harm you, then you will become fearful, self-suspicious, disempowered and controlling. If, on the other hand, you assume that this part of you is acting for what it sees as your own best interest, then you will be more empowered to raise your awareness and to deal with it more constructively and effectively.

Possible factors involved in procrastination

- Your heart's reluctance to do something which is not right for you
- You have agreed to something half-heartedly and are dragging your feet
- Your belief patterns are in conflict with your moving forward
- You are not ready to leave the security of your established 'comfort zone'
- Your unconscious mind puts immediate relief or gratification ahead of long term rewards.

When a goal is not right for you, or you don't really care about it, you operate from 'shoulds' and the process is likely to be an unfulfilling struggle. If you have had some goal or intention on your list for ages, without making any real progress, start by asking yourself if deep down you really want it that much. If it has simply become a 'should' then let it go.

If you have agreed with somebody else to do it, then either talk with them and re-negotiate or else fully accept that you have given your word and complete it. What seldom works is to put your head in the sand and to hope that it will go away.

Reflection point   **Letting go of the 'shoulds'**

What goal or projects are you now ready to let go of?

Who else is involved and what do you need to say to them?

If you are obliged to stick to an agreement, are you now ready to accept responsibility and to follow through on it?

If, after reflection, you do really want a goal and yet you still find yourself stuck, and up against some deep inner resistance, then it is likely that there are some underlying beliefs or assumptions that are getting in the way. The different approaches to changing limiting beliefs, explored in chapter 4, will be helpful.

Reflection point   **Beliefs that block goals**

In relation to a particular goal or project, what might you be assuming that is preventing you from moving forward with it?

What would be a more freeing assumption, that is real for you?

Taking on board this new assumption, what will you now do to move forward?

Beliefs, with associated feelings and ways of looking at things, form your attitudes to yourself, life and possibility. They are maintained by the reaction cycles described in chapter 2, which you may like to look at again. As well as questioning and changing your assumptions, you will need to support this with changes in the other two parts of the cycle — namely, how you behave and express yourself and how you formulate your experience. All of this entails moving outside your present comfort zone.

By definition, moving outside the security of your established comfort zone always involves some form of discomfort and frequently brings up anxiety, whether you think it is justified or not. Recognising and accepting that this is what is happening can help you to 'feel the fear and do it anyway'. Useful approaches include chunking the goal down into smaller aspects that are not so daunting and, where possible, getting some outside support.

Reflection point **Moving outside your comfort zone**

What goals or projects are you procrastinating on so that you don't have to move outside your comfort zone?

Are you now ready to go through the discomfort, feel the fear and do it anyway?

What support do you need to do this?

Even when the goal is right for you, and you have no deeper resistance, you may still find yourself procrastinating. The problem is that your unconscious mind tends to look for immediate comfort now, even when that means postponing necessary action and sabotaging future worthwhile results. Whatever shouts loudest in the moment gets attention even if, in the background, disasters are waiting to happen. You may be dangerously overweight and set goals for improved health and fitness. In the moment, though, you find that your positive intentions are over-ruled when desire for a chocolate biscuit shouts louder. For these situations, as well as to support more radical changes in the belief cycle, you can use different techniques for following through.

Following through techniques

Firstly, it is important to realize that not doing what you said you would do does not mean that you are a bad person or that you are inherently lazy or incapable. Your unconscious mind is simply responding to what shouts loudest in the moment. To get round this, you need to consciously create strategies and structures so that, in the moment, what you want to happen makes more noise. You have to set things up so that it is easier to choose behaviours that support your intentions than to ignore them. An everyday example of this is getting up in the morning to go to work. You could just say that, because you know it is important, you will do it and that if you don't then it just means that you are lazy and must try harder. In practice, though, you use an alarm clock because otherwise the short term attraction of the warm duvet is likely to win out over the long term benefits of keeping a job! The alarm serves two purposes: firstly, it reminds you of what you have chosen to do; secondly, the noise it makes means that it is now more comfortable to get up and switch it off than to stay in bed.

In line with the alarm clock example, there are a number of techniques for giving more support to your longer term intentions, so that they are not forgotten or pushed aside in the short term.

The two main elements for following through successfully:

1. Keeping the intention in mind
2. Making it easier to choose the long term intention than to ignore it with:
    - Positive consequences that reward desired behaviour
    - Negative consequences for ignoring it
    - A combination of positive and negative consequences

Ways of keeping the intention in mind include writing notes for yourself, getting other people to remind you, and keeping some kind of visual record. The method suggested in chapter 2 was to write your intention down. Then, twice per day, subjectively score yourself out of ten for how much you kept to your intention, as well as making a note of any relevant factors.

That may be enough or you may want to add weight to it by adding some consequences. These can be minor or, if needed, you can increase them.

When clients in sales procrastinate about making calls to potential customers, I often give them the positive consequence fieldwork of counting the 'No's' they receive, and rewarding themselves for a certain number. Provided that they take action, they then win either way. If the prospect says 'Yes' then they get the business and if the prospect says 'No' then they are one step closer to the reward. It makes the whole thing much lighter and more of a game.

I prefer to emphasize positive consequences and use negative consequences sparingly. They are, though, a part of life and can sometimes be highly effective motivators, provided that you do not use them to belittle yourself or to imply that you are a bad person. Negative consequences need to be clearly set up and agreed beforehand. Then, when they are applied and accepted, you are free to learn and start again. In the bigger picture, the consequences are then just another tool to help you achieve the things that really matter to you.

Outcomes for self-coaching

When clients start a course of coaching, I usually suggest that they begin with looking at the overall balance of their life. From this perspective, they can then clarify their three-year vision and set some one-year and three-months goals. I also ask them to consider how, in the first three months, they will increase their sources of positive energy and eliminate some of their energy drains (see chapter 3).

On the next page is a structure you can use for yourself. You can download it as a *Word* document from the members' section at www.self-factor.com.

The eight spokes represent a balanced wheel. Take the centre or hub of the wheel as 0 (totally dissatisfied) and the outer edge as 10 (totally satisfied). Rank your level of satisfaction in each area by putting a cross on the relevant spoke. Draw lines to join the crosses. The less balanced

WHEEL OF LIFE BALANCE

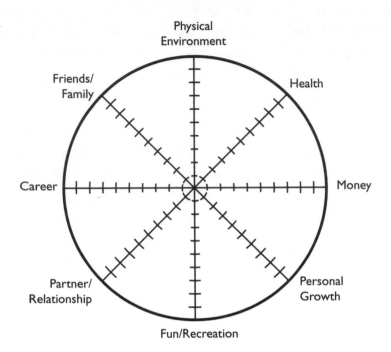

your wheel is, the more wobbly will be your ride through life. The more balanced the wheel is, the smoother it will run.

How balanced is your life? Where do you need to make changes? Record your scores so that you can come back to them and monitor progress.

Wheel of Life Balance scores on date: _____ / _____ / _____

Environment	Health	Money	Personal Growth
Fun/ Recreation	Partnership	Career	Friends/ Family

Three-year vision

Describe how you want your life to look and feel in 3 years from now, so as to be ideal for you.

_____

_____

_____

_____

_____

One-year goals

Make a list of 3-6 goals for the next year which support you in moving towards your three-year vision. These can be 'doing', 'learning' or 'being' goals. Choose three of these to be your primary goals for the year.

Primary one-year goals:

1. _____

2. _____

3. _____

Other one-year goals:

4. _____

5. _____

6. _____

Three-month goals

Make a list of 3-6 goals for the next three months which support you in moving towards your primary one-year goals. Again, choose three of these to be your primary focus. Pick goals you really want and not those you think you ought or might want. Start with goals that you feel really motivated and ready to move forward with.

Primary three-month goals:

1. _____

2. _____

3. _____

Other three-month goals:

4. _____

5. _____

6. _____

Energy-building over the next three months

List what you will do or put in place to nourish yourself and boost your energy, including positive daily habits.

_____

_____

_____

_____

_____

Energy drains to clear in the next three months

Make a list of energy drains to clear in the next three months.

_____

_____

_____

_____

_____

As you take action towards your goals, you will get feedback in the light of which you can update your vision and goals. It will be helpful to revisit and revise your coaching outcomes every three months or so.

8 ~ Working with Organizations

Here is an overview of some of the ways in which coaching, and related approaches, are being used in organizations.

You get professional life coaches and you also get professional business or executive coaches. Some, like myself, work in both spheres. In practice, whichever area coaching is used in, the foundations are the same because you are dealing with people. The coach listens and asks questions to help the client raise their awareness and responsibility, tap into their own resources and wisdom, generate their own solutions and then take action. Maintaining a resourceful state and taking an empowered stance are essential for everyone, whatever they are doing. It is equally important that you stay connected, with yourself and your truth, and support yourself through the ups and downs that are a part of both life and business. Much of business coaching involves some element of personal coaching and it is often the case that the challenges showing up in a client's business life are reflections of the challenges that show up in their personal life.

The first and most important way to use coaching principles, to help your organization, is to apply them to yourself. If you have a strong relationship with, and sense of, self then you will be more effective at whatever you are doing. From this place, you can then support others in realizing and expressing their own potential.

The people factor

Just as the SELF-factor is the foundation for a healthy and successful individual, so the people factor is the foundation for a healthy and successful organization. The progress of an organization depends largely on the resourcefulness and effectiveness of the people involved. There are a number of different ways in which coaching, and related approaches, can be implemented to utilize and develop the people factor.

Individual coaching

When an executive, or other member of an organization, receives individual coaching then it can be set up in a number of ways including:

- The client arranges and pays for coaching themselves
  - This leaves the client free to set the agenda and to work on both personal and work areas. They can also use the coaching for career planning, whether within or outside their present organization.
- The client arranges coaching and the organization pays all or part of the fees
  - The client is again free to set the agenda, although they may have discussed this with their organization.
- The organization contracts an external coach to work with individuals
  - This only works if the individual client wants coaching and sees the benefit for themselves. In this case, the agenda is usually jointly agreed with the client, the organization and the coach. It may be agreed that other issues, important to the client, can also be looked at provided that the joint agenda is not forgotten.
- The organization uses its own internal coaches to work with individuals
  - This can work well provided that confidentiality and other

boundaries are clarified and agreed at the outset. The remit of an internal coach is usually narrower and focused solely on enhancing work performance. Sometimes clients may be reluctant to express their doubts or problems with someone from their own organization, and feel freer when working with an external coach.

Individual coaching is often done by telephone. This makes it much more time-efficient and allows the client to be in touch with the coach wherever they are. Like many other coaches, I now do most of my work by phone and have an international client base.

Coaching and training

Coaching can be used in the way that training is delivered and it can also be used to complement training and to make it more effective. Trainers who use a coaching approach will make their courses more interactive and tend to build on the participants' own experience and ideas. The more that participants are involved in generating new ideas and procedures, the more likely they are to take responsibility for making them work when the time comes to apply them for real. It is also becoming increasingly common for trainings to be supplemented by follow-up, individual coaching. This gives participants support in applying the material and in dealing with the practical challenges that invariably crop up.

Developing a coaching culture

At its heart, coaching, as I apply it, is a way of interacting with yourself, your life and your business from a responsible, positive and pro-active point of view. It supports you in appreciating people, building on their strengths and making the best of shared opportunities. When organizations incorporate this approach they become more pleasant places in which to work, as well as becoming more effective.

Coaching skills for managers and executives

One of the most effective ways to promote a coaching culture is to train managers and executives in this approach. To a certain extent, this happens by osmosis when they themselves are coached over an extended period of time and, seeing the benefits, start to apply some of what they have experienced with their teams. Alongside this, many organizations, as well as business colleges, now provide, or buy in, coaching skills training for managers. The manager, as coach, is more able to empower individuals and to develop better teams.

Appreciative Inquiry

This is an innovative approach to organizational visioning and strategy which has a similar perspective to coaching. Appreciative Inquiry is most effective when it involves the entire workforce, from board members to people on the shop floor. Rather than starting by focusing on what is wrong in an organization, it looks for what is already good and gives the organization its vitality. Building on this, it then establishes a shared, desired vision. And then come the shared strategy and action plans, which are again created with everybody's input. This approach creates a positive 'we can do it' feel. Also, the fact that people have been jointly involved in creating a vision and strategy means that they are far more likely to be fully behind it and to make it work. Appreciative Inquiry has been used successfully by a very diverse range of organizations including multi-nationals, small businesses, schools and colleges, charities and aid organizations. The Dalai Lama used it as the basis for an ecumenical meeting of religious leaders and, in Nepal, it was used as the main approach for a women's literacy program involving over 200,000 women.

Following through in companies

When we looked at individual goal-setting and action plans, we saw how easy it can be to ignore what you know and have agreed needs doing. That is why you need structures which, like your alarm clock in the morning, both remind you of your intention and provide immediate incentive to follow through on it. The same applies to being a manager in an organization. Many feedback systems are incomplete and don't give feedback quickly enough to allow you to make necessary changes in present time.

One tool that my associates have developed to help with this is an ongoing computer-based feedback system for managers of all levels. It monitors overall performance as well as showing how this is being influenced by different factors. If there is a dip in performance, you can immediately check which factors may be involved and remedy them early on. Consultants first spend time, together with the managers involved, identifying key performance factors. These can include hard measurements as well as softer, subjective elements — such as quality of communication and individual satisfaction. Then they set up and install the feedback system. For this to work, it is essential to get full buy-in from the managers so that they see it and respond to it as a positive support tool. Hence, it works best with a coaching approach.

If you would like more information on any of the services mentioned in this chapter, then you can contact us via the web site at www.self-factor.com.

Further Resources

At the web site, www.self-factor.com, you can find a list of books and other resources. There is also a members' section which has a variety of forms, audio recordings, guided visualizations and other tools that complement the material in this book.

At the same site, you can find out more about coaching services offered by the author and associates.

About the Author

Duncan works with a variety of international clients and trains and mentors coaches from the UK, Europe, USA, Canada and Australia. As well as running his own coaching business, he is a mentor coach and assessor for other UK coaching companies and a Coach Trainer and Professional Mentor Coach with Coach U International. He coaches one-to-one and in groups, and writes a newsletter on coaching-related topics. He also speaks, on coaching-related topics, to organizations and conferences.

Together with his associate coaches, and other professionals, Duncan provides a range of coaching services for individuals and organizations including:

- Life Coaching
- Leadership and Executive Coaching
- Coach Training and Mentoring
- Other Trainings with a Coaching Perspective

- Appreciative Inquiry for Organizational Visioning and
  Planning
- Feedback Systems for Management Performance
  Improvement

To find out more, visit www.self-factor.com

or send an email to info@self-factor.com